Multimedia Marketing
for Design Firms

Multimedia Marketing for Design Firms

Curtis B. Charles
Karen M. Brown

Liz
Thank you for your
Continued support

JOHN WILEY & SONS, INC.

New York • Chichester • Brisbane • Toronto • Singapore

This publication is designed to provide accurate and authoritative information in regard to the subject matter covered. It is sold with the understanding that the publisher is not engaged in rendering legal, accounting, or other professional services. If legal advice or other expert assistance is required, the services of a competent professional person should be sought.

Library of Congress Cataloging-in-Publication Data

Charles, Curtis B.
    Multimedia marketing for design firms / Curtis B. Charles and
Karen M. Brown.
        p.   cm.
    Includes index.
    ISBN 0-471-14609-9 (pbk. : alk. paper)
    1. Architectural services marketing--United States--Data
processing.   I. Brown, Karen M.   II. Title.
NA1996.5.C48   1996
720'.285--dc20   96-13838

Printed in the United States of America

10 9 8 7 6 5 4 3 2 1

This book is dedicated to the memories of
Professor Lloyd Harris, Artist, Trinidad/St. Kitts
and
Dr. Kei Mori, Scientist, Tokyo, Japan

and to our daughters Khadijah and Felicia
for their patience, understanding, and encouragement throughout this project

Foreword

This book is founded on the exploration and experience of individuals in both academia and private practice. It describes the enormous potential of computing to benefit the world of architecture and design. *Multimedia Marketing for Design Firms* takes a thorough look at the potential of new communication tools as encountered by the authors and some of their colleagues. Desktop publishing, computer visualization—such as 3D modeling, rendering, animation, VRML, and QuickTime VR—the Internet, and multimedia combinations are all covered with user-friendly instructions.

As in many other fields, computer innovation among designers is a dialectic between academic and professional efforts. The case studies presented here are primarily from the professional world because that is where marketing material is developed. However, they provide a framework of information which can be as useful for students as it is for professionals; anecdotal experiences from the profession provide a combination of theory and practice which is also effective in the academic setting. I am pleased to introduce you to this very useful book, and do so with encouragement for your success in assimilating its advice.

ELIZABETH PLATER-ZYBERK
Architect
Dean, University of Miami
School of Architecture

This book is essential reading for all who need to be on the front edge of the multimedia marketing curve. Curtis Charles and Karen Brown have written an informed and concept-filled book that will support the efforts of all who are interested in understanding the alignment of the electronic environment and contemporary business practices.

The time has passed when businesses at any level can ignore the necessity of having Internet Web sites—a major connection with local and global markets. The number of enterprises that are electronically intelligent has grown geometrically; no longer are there a select few on the World Wide Web. On the contrary, a position in the electronic information access/transmission milieu is a basic infrastructure requirement for business development and client service.

The computer, which once was simply a means to access data, has developed into a powerful tool for communicating multiple layers of ideas and information. In addition to interfacing client needs with consultant abilities, powerful notebook hardware systems provide immediate and unlimited access to and transmission of creative responses to any design problem.

This second book from Charles and Brown brings transparency to the value of multimedia marketing and the use of advanced computer technology and sophisticated software. For those who are considering an investment in communication and marketing technology, this book is worth reading.

HARRY G. ROBINSON III, FAIA AICP
Vice President for Academic Affairs
Howard University

C·O·N·T·E·N·T·S

1

DESKTOP PUBLISHING   3

2

VISUALIZATION TOOLS 31

3

DESKTOP DIGITAL VIDEO 97

4

5

6 DELIVERY MEDIA 177

7 MULTIMEDIA MARKETING IN ACTION 207

Creative labs ShareVision

Preface

Marketing is an essential ingredient in any business recipe. Informing potential customers about your business and the services you offer is the key to the survival of that business. If you are the only one who knows what you can do, then you will not have a business. As a result, a significant portion of a company's resources must be dedicated to acquiring new clients.

Advances in technology have brought change to almost all business activity in every profession including architecture. The computer is thought of as the great equalizer among similar business types of different sizes. It has allowed smaller firms to compete with large firms on a more equal footing by automating many tasks that, prior to the availability of computer technology, would have required a much larger staff to achieve.

Until now, you have no doubt used traditional marketing media—letters and brochures, phone calls, flyers, newspaper ads, and video. In this electronic age, we have new tools for marketing—e-mail, video conferencing, portable documents on diskettes, home pages on the Internet, and interactive multimedia.

Electronic mail (e-mail) gets your letter there immediately instead of in a few days via the postal service. Flyers and brochures can be distributed on diskette in the portable document format (PDF). This means that your clients can see your material on their own computers, in color, just as you created it, even though they do not have the software program that you used to create it.

The computer station you now use to do computer-aided design and drafting (CADD) can help you create a variety of marketing presentations with new software purchases and only minor upgrades in hardware. The more adventurous can purchase systems that will let you create full-fledged multimedia and desktop video presentations.

Instead of trying to explain your concept over the telephone, you can video conference with your client and share files on screen so both offices can discuss the project, see the changes immediately on the screen, and wrap up the issues quickly. You can transform your video into an interactive multimedia presentation, allowing your clients to choose what will be seen according to their particular interest. You can include text, graphics, video, and audio for a new and exciting way to present your work. The electronic version of the newspaper is the Internet. The information superhighway, as it's often called, offers new marketing and research opportunities to give your office the competitive edge.

In this new and exciting electronic age, desktop marketing is full of opportunities and challenges for businesses. The purpose of this book is to show you how to adapt and use this new technology to give yourself an advantage.

Acknowledgments

This book was laid out and designed electronically by the authors, Curtis B. Charles and Karen M. Brown, principals of C4 Studio. All graphics for the Tips and Tricks section of Chapter 1, pp. 12–28, were created by LeftRight Studios, Miami; Allen Welker and Rowena Luna, principals. Research assistance was provided by Alejandro Santamariá, Rafael Tapanes, Simone Christian, and Shirley Franco, students at the University of Miami School of Architecture. Analytical computer-generated models and renderings were produced by C4 Studios and by students attending a computer visualization course taught by Curtis Charles at the University of Miami School of Architecture.

The generous support of cutting-edge companies like IBM, Apple, Adobe, Macromedia, Autodesk, Microsoft, Autodessys, Inc., InFocus, FWB Inc., Phillips, Strata 3D, Texas Instruments, Calcomp, Bentley Systems, Graphisoft Inc., and Avid Technolgies made it possible for us to present the most advanced technologies to you in the form of this book and CD-ROM.

Illustration Credits

Page x (top): Derrick Walker
Chapter Openers: C4 Studio/Reneè Green
Pages 34–35: Douglas West
Page 37: C4 Studio
Pages 41–43: Graphisoft U.S., Inc.
Pages 57–60: Gustavo Cardon
Page 61: Ramon Lastra
Pages 62–63: Brion M. Kean
Page 64: Jose M. Bofill
Page 65: Rodrigo Reyes
Pages 66–75: C4 Studio
Page 79: Douglas West
Page 80: Carolin Butz
Pages 85–86: Apple Computer
Page 90 (bottom): Graphisoft U.S., Inc.
Page 91: Graphisoft U.S., Inc.
Page 109: C4 Studio

Multimedia Marketing for Design Firms

Desktop Publishing

Chapter 1

B y now, the term desktop publishing (DTP) is a familiar one. Walk into any major bookstore and you are sure to find a vibrant section dedicated to the topic. Desktop publishing incorporates text and graphics to create striking marketing and promotional documents of varying complexity right on your computer. Today, with a page layout application and some practice, you can literally perform the combined duties of graphic artist, designer, composer, editor, pasteup artist, and typographer.

Before the advent of desktop publishing, design firms depended on public relations and graphic design firms to produce most of their marketing materials, an expensive practice for many firms. Aldus Corporation (now Adobe Systems Incorporated), introduced desktop publishing to the

masses through its flagship product, PageMaker, around the same time Apple Computer introduced the Macintosh computer. This combination changed forever the way documents were created. Desktop publishing has taken marketing duties away from large agencies and put the task back into the hands of the architectural firm, where it belongs.

Architects are trained problem solvers—we take a design problem, we analyze it, synthesize it, and come up with a design solution. I believe we can solve any design problem, whether it be the design of a building or the design of marketing documents to be distributed to potential clients. This is not a new concept—remember, architects trained in the Bauhaus system designed every visual component associated with the building. For example, an architect who designed a restaurant would have also designed the signage, menu, napkins, as well as all communication materials for the owner to market the restaurant to potential customers. Therefore, based on our training as problem solvers, it is conceivable that architects conducting marketing duties in a firm can very well be composer, editor, pasteup artist and typographer. After all, these duties involve the solution of a design problem: how to employ desktop publishing tools in order to create marketing communications for the purpose of attracting clients.

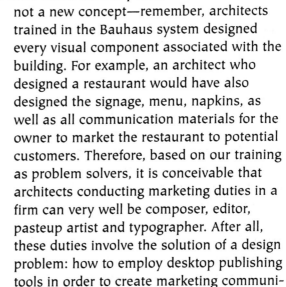

Many of you have used some sort of desktop publishing techniques to create your business and personnel documents: those flyers with clip art graphics that you made for the company picnic, business documents and forms, and your company

Text	Graphics
Word processor	Illustration applications
Scanned documents	Scanned images
OCR (Optical Character Recognition)	Clip art
	CAD programs
	Visualization programs

brochure are all examples of desktop publishing, created using text and graphics applications and composed in a page layout application. The text and graphics used may originate from a variety of sources, summarized in the table shown here.

TEXT

Word Processing

Typing was probably one of the first office tasks to be automated. Early word processors were expensive but offered advantages the typewriter could not match. It brought efficiency to the office, similar to the efficiency gains realized when architects welcomed computer-aided design (CAD) into their offices. Users input documents once then make changes without having to redo the entire document.

Today's premier word processing applications have those same basic features and then some. You can now fiddle with text, place graphics, charts or tables, and link to database information, all within one package.

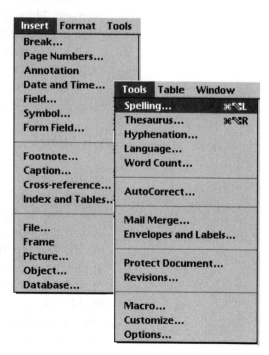

Your word processing application will be the primary source of text for your marketing documents. It has a strong suite of tools to make typing a breeze. It will check your spelling and grammar, and offer suggestions about your choice of words from its thesaurus. It will copy and paste text from another word processing document, change text sizes and characteristics—**bold**, *italics*, <u>underline</u>, and more—adjust text alignment, set headers and footnotes, and employ style sheets to ensure consistency in your office documentation.

Scanned Documents

OCR, or Optical Character Recognition, will allow you to use your scanner to digitize text that may not already be on your computer. The scanner uses OCR to read text into your computer. It saves having to retype documents and, once the text is in your computer, it behaves the same as if you had typed it in yourself. Thus, you can edit it in your word processor prior to placing it in your page layout application.

Another twist on OCR is its use with faxed documents. OCR will read your faxed documents directly into the word processing application.

GRAPHICS

Illustration

Illustration packages allow you to create digital art for your marketing documents. The top illustration applications on the market provide an array of tools that enable you to create almost any two-dimensional shape your mind can conceive. You can

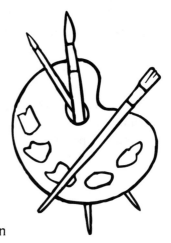

manipulate different shapes, use different fills, patterns, and colors. You can also work with text to create stylized titles using techniques such as mapping text to paths.

Many illustration applications work with layers, a familiar look and feel for those of you who work with CAD. The layers allow you to experiment with different ideas during the creative process, somewhat similar to using bumwah for demonstrating different design solutions.

Scanned Images

A scanner will allow you to add graphic images, not already on your computer, to your documents. You can scan images such as sketches and project photographs and logos for inclusion in your marketing materials. Color or black and white, all your images can now be included. Used in conjunction with image-editing software, the possibilities are limitless. With Adobe's Photoshop, you can edit images; apply filters and special effects such as watercolor, charcoal, and color pencil; combine models of proposed buildings with photos of the site to create a photo montage.

Clip Art

Clip art consists mostly of line art, ready-made for your use. It is usually organized into categories such as business, medical, construction, and so on. These graphics can be placed directly onto your document where appropriate to add excitement or illustrate a point. You can purchase the clip art library that most suits your needs.

CAD and Visualization

Looking at your CAD program, under the file menu, you'll find an Export or Save As command that will allow you to save individual drawing sheets as files that can then be imported into a page layout program.

Your three-dimensional model can also be saved as a separate digital file for inclusion in your marketing documents.

If your CAD or visualization programs do not allow you to save your files in a format that can be accepted by your page layout application, do not despair. I have another option for you. You can use a screen capture utility to take a "snapshot" of the screen. The utility will save the picture, usually in a pict file format to your hard drive. You can then import it into your page layout or use DeBabelizer to convert it if necessary. This will allow you to take pictures of the project for inclusion in your marketing material.

TIPS AND TRICKS

The creation of any desktop publishing piece can involve many stages and, depending on the task at hand, could mean the use of more than one software package. Illustration, image editing and page layout are all steps on the way to the completion of desktop documents. It is rare that you use just one application to fulfill all your needs. Graphics

have to be created; preexisting images cleaned up and stylized; text has to be spell-checked and edited. None of these tasks can be adequately accomplished using a single software package. With that in mind, instead of looking at these applications individually, we will look at how they can be used in combination to complete some of the tasks you may want to accomplish in your office.

It is important to note that, while there are many applications that can be used, the applications chosen here were selected for two main reasons:

- Their excellent array of tools, which help to ensure that the only limit to what you can create is your own imagination.
- They are industry standards, which facilitate the easy movement of files between applications as well as to service bureaus. Many people have been caught using a package that creates files that are proprietary and cannot be exported to or imported from other applications. The following presentations illustrate graphically the way you would utilize these different applications in the completion of a project, taking past projects and incorporating them into a brochure for marketing purposes.

Adobe PageMaker and QuarkXPress are the two big guns in the page layout category.

The premier image-editing application on the market today is Adobe Photoshop.

FreeHand and Adobe Illustrator are competitors in the field of graphic design and illustration.

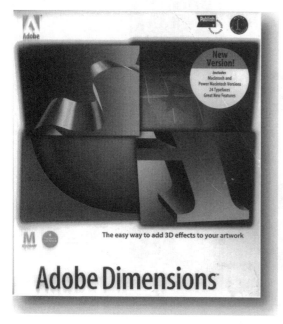

Adobe Dimensions is used to create specialized 3-dimensional effects.

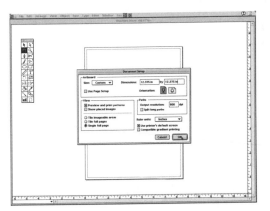

Set up Illustrator document to include bleed area.

Create rough object shape using pen tool.

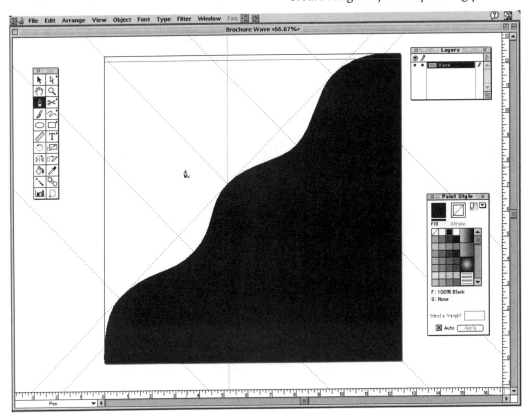

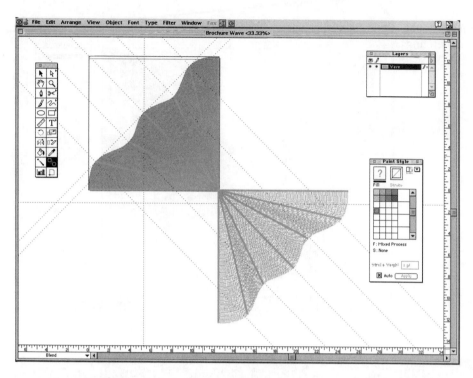

Fine-tune the object through the use of Bezier curves.
Copy and rotate the object 180 degrees and fill the second object with white.
Use the blend tool on two corresponding points of the object.

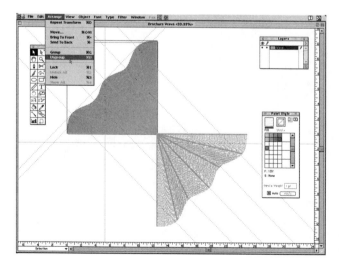

Ungroup and delete
the unwanted objects
from the blend function.

The final object,
ready for rasterizing.

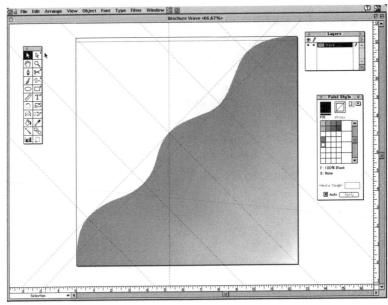

PHASE II - PHOTOSHOP 3.0.4

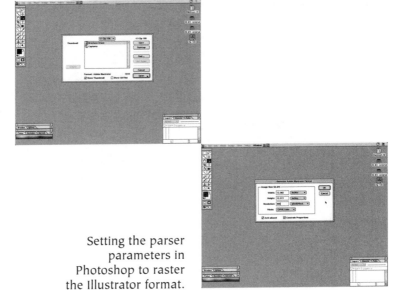

Opening the
wave file from
Illustrator format.

Setting the parser
parameters in
Photoshop to raster
the Illustrator format.

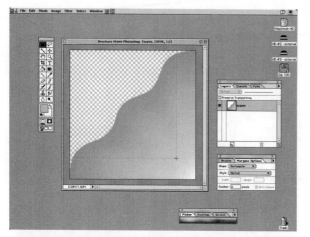

Select all with the marquee tool.

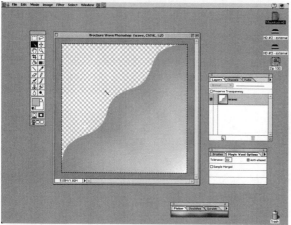

Deselect the unwanted area with the wand tool.

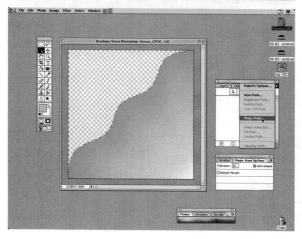

Select the MAKE PATH command under the path palette submenu.

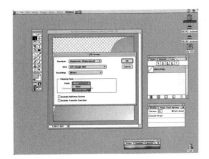

Save image in EPS format
with the clipping path option.

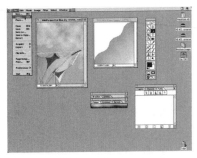

Open the clipped wave file
and the file containing
the inset photograph.

Create a NEW LAYER in the clipped file.
Make sure it is under the layer
containing the clipping path.

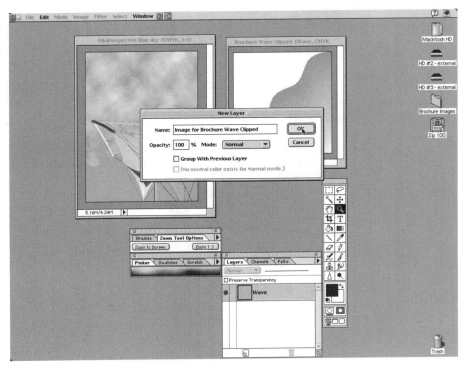

Delete the pixels of the wave, leaving only the clipping path.

COPY-PASTE the inset photograph into the layer under the clipping path.

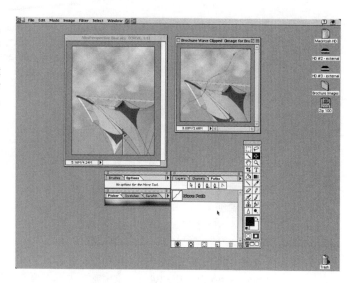

Position image and select area to be duplicated to fill the required space.

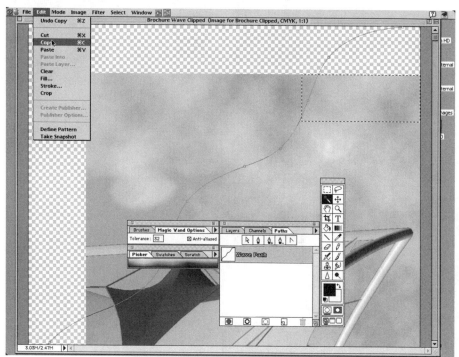

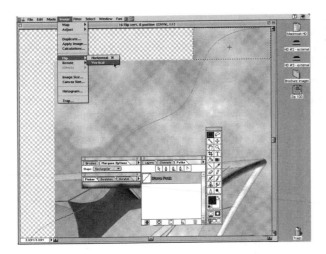

Float the selected area and drag copy to new area. Vertical flip the selection and position in place.

Save as an EPS file with the clipping path option.

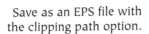

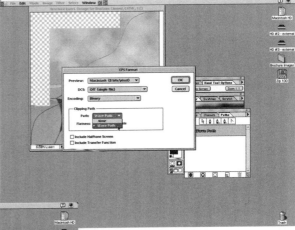

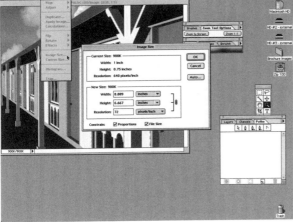

Using the IMAGE SIZE command to resize, and save each supporting image as an EPS file.

Set up the document parameters.

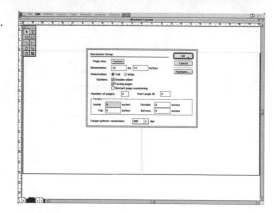

Place the first image on the page.

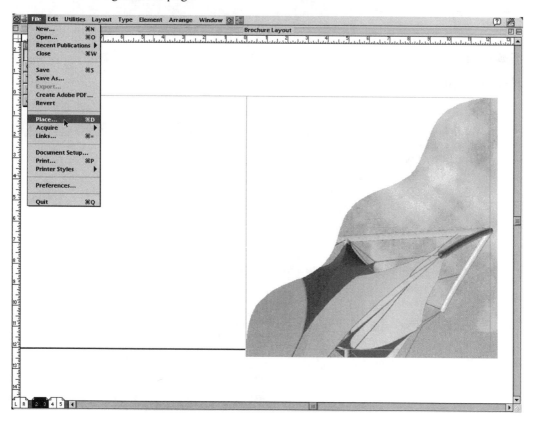

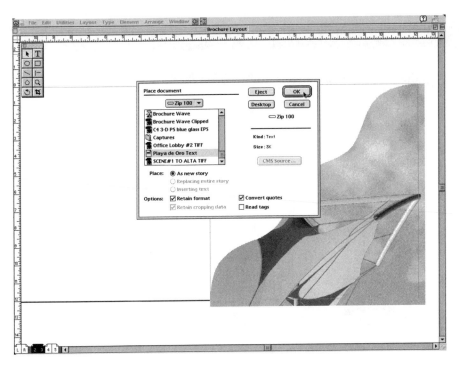

Place text in a text box.

Apply a drop cap to the first character of the body text.

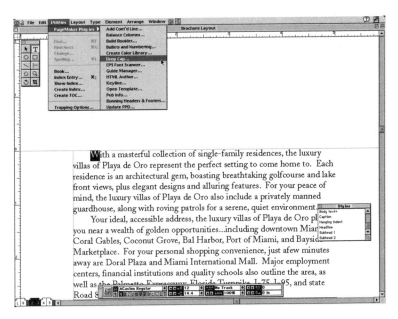

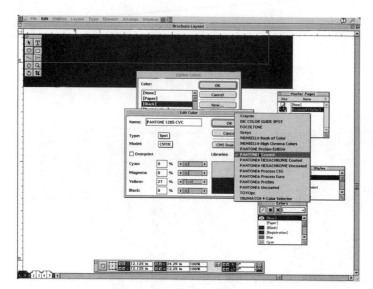

Add specific colors
to the color palette.

In the DEFINE COLORS
dialog box, click EDIT
COLOR to bring up the
EDIT COLOR dialog box.
Choose a color system
from the Libraries
submenu or enter
exact numerical values.

Place the remaining
document elements in
the same way and voilà!

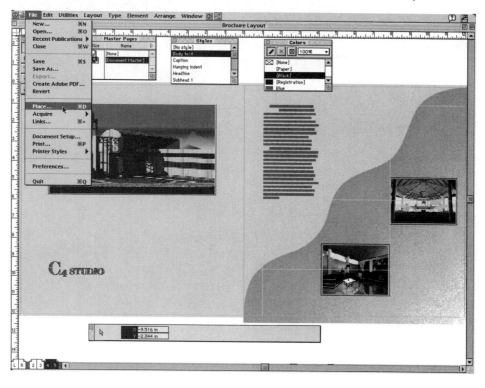

C44 STUDIO

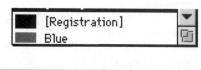

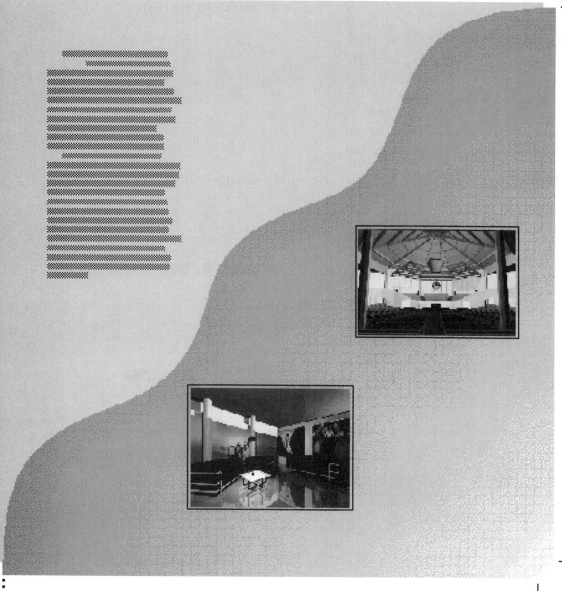

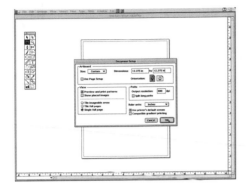

Lay out type for logo and set to actual size, and save as an EPS file.

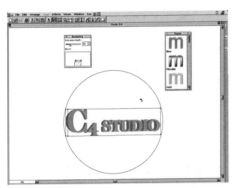

Open and rotate the EPS file to the desired perspective.

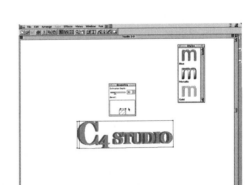

Set bevel and extrusion depth.

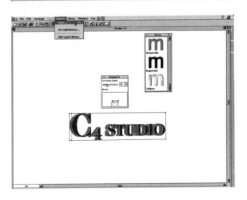

Apply styles and color.

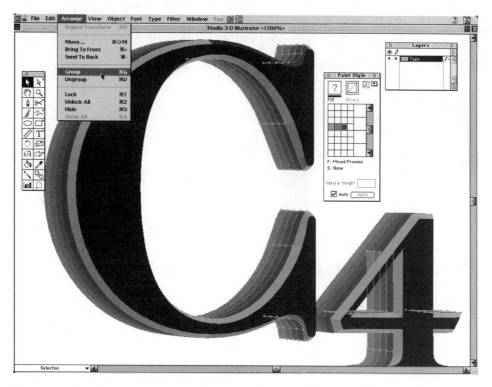

Group object subsets, create new layers, and save in Illustrator format.

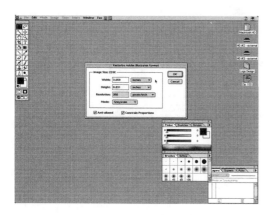

Use Photoshop to rasterize Illustrator file to desired size and resolution,
select and create clipping path, and save as an EPS file.

Letterhead

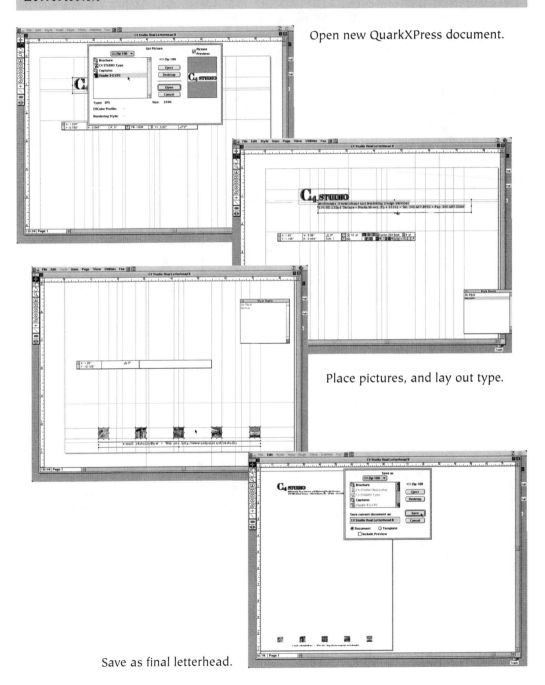

Open new QuarkXPress document.

Place pictures, and lay out type.

Save as final letterhead.

Envelope

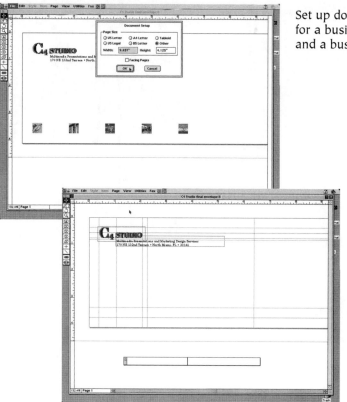

Set up document parameters for a business-sized envelope and a business card.

Then place pictures and lay out type.

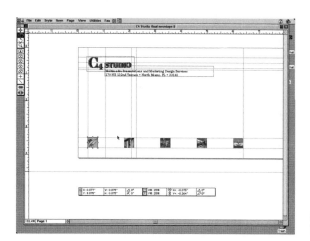

Save as final envelope and business card respectively.

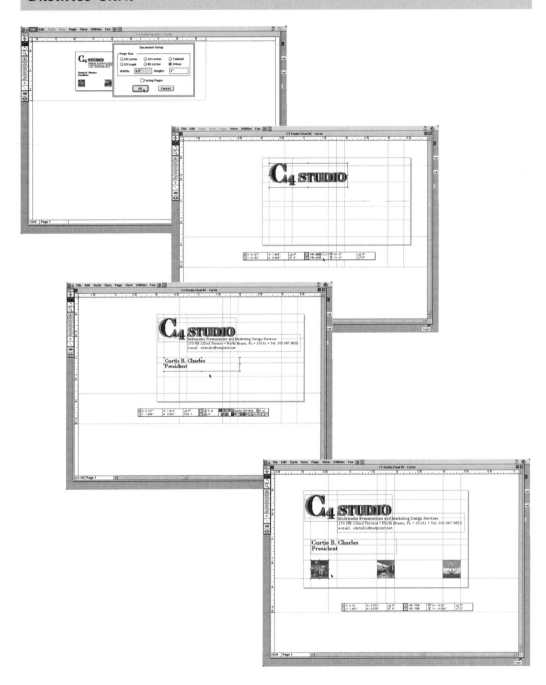

The preceding illustrates graphically, the way in which you can use a combination of software applications to create some of your presentations. Files originally created in one application moved seamlessly to other applications for further refining until the entire project came together. This is the essence of desktop publishing—the power of the software tools illustrated to create and display your vision for a project.

Chapter 2

Architects have always used visual aids to communicate their design ideas. Nowhere in the history of architecture is this more evident than during the Renaissance period where perspective drawings were the primary medium used to express and communicate the three-dimensional nature of architectural designs. Today, an architect may still sketch on a napkin during a luncheon meeting. However, since even the simplest of designs can be incomprehensible to the average client, we must continue to search for new and innovative visualization techniques.

Typically, architects use floor plans, elevations, site plans, and beautiful watercolor renderings when

marketing their services to potential clients. We mount these drawings on boards or present our designs using slides and overhead transparencies. What we fail to recognize is that these traditional techniques are discussed in architectural jargon, understood only by other architects. In many instances, it is a foreign language to clients, tantamount to dropping someone in a country where the language and customs are unfamiliar and saying "survive for a week!" The struggle to understand the customs and language can be an insurmountable task for that person. When marketing design services, our role should be that of translator and communicator.

It is becoming more difficult to convince clients to utilize our design services by making traditional marketing presentations since clients are becoming more diverse; they are aware of and accustomed to the use of technology in every facet of their existence. Firms are forced to compete fiercely for projects and turn around sketches in a matter of days. In such a situation, larger firms have traditionally held a competitive advantage, as they could outspend their smaller competitors. Creative use of visualization technology levels the playing field somewhat for smaller companies.

C4 Studio, our 3D visualization firm, works with architects to improve communication and win design commissions. One of our clients, a seven-person architectural firm, is comprised of two partners, one project manager, two CAD operators and two administration personnel. During the past 12 months, C4 Studio served as 3D visualization consultant on three projects. Before each presentation, we would meet with the principal to discuss the design program, presentation strategy and, develop a storyboard. Once sketches were completed, C4 Studio's task was to create computer-generated models and virtual animation sequences showing the architecture firm's strategy to address the design concerns of the client as well as the unique design issues that the proposed design project presented. For each of the three design competitions for which we provided 3D visualization services, the architect won the commission, beating out much larger architecture firms. In one instance, one of the competing firms had 200 employees, proving once again that bigger is not always better.

This client is a typical example of the use of 3D visualization as a marketing tool. Instead of trying to explain a 2D solution, the client was shown a three-dimensional model that clearly depicted architectural themes and massed relationships within the project and among other structures throughout the site. This presentation was easily understood by the client and conveyed an understanding of the issues that the project presented.

Clearly, 3D visualization, not the size of the firm, was the determining factor in winning this design commission. No longer can we expect the client to guess at the grand design ideas circulating in our heads. No longer can we afford to use only sketches and blue-printed orthographic drawings to convey our design ideas to a client who has ready money to hire an architect, and who yearns to comprehend your solutions. If you want to continue to be competitive, you must invest in and embrace the technology because, as illustrated, if you don't, your competitor will. It's as simple as that.

WHAT IS COMPUTER VISUALIZATION?

Computer visualization is a technique used in architecture design that enables others to clearly understand our ideas and concepts, be they design professionals or laypeople. While traditional visualization techniques include cardboard models and artistic renderings, computer visualization enhances traditional techniques by expanding the possibilities. Instead of a static cardboard model, you can have a photorealistically rendered computer model, complete with actual materials, lighting,

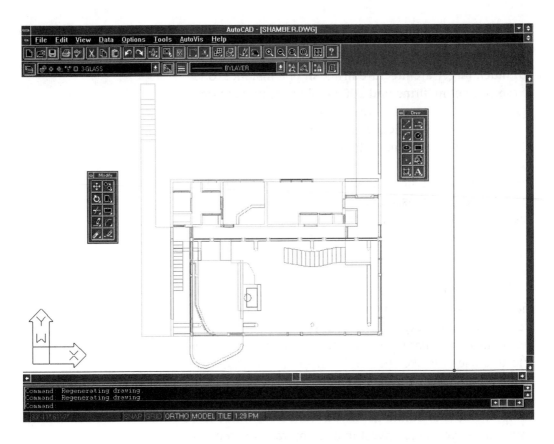

Step 1 Prepare 2D drawings for the generation of a 3D model for
Richard Meier's Shamberg House using Autodesk's AutoCAD.

texture, furniture, people, and atmosphere. Instead of
a single, static rendering, you can experience an animated
walkthrough.

    With the advent of Intel-based personal computers in
1980 a small group of pioneers began to develop visualization software. This first group of visualization applications such as Topas and RIO was designed primarily for
broadcast graphics, and never reached the architecture

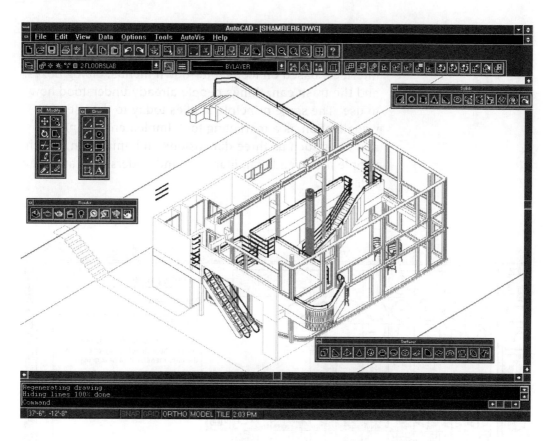

Step 2 Familiarity with the same environment that created the 2D drawing in Step 1, coupled with the new, user-friendly solid and surface modeling tools of Autodesk's AutoCAD, made the generation of this 3D model of Richard Meier's Shamberg House easy to accomplish.

firm even though they had tremendous potential for the practice of architecture.

It was not until 1984, with Apple Computer's introduction of the Macintosh that visualization software applicable to the practice of architecture became accessible to the profession. Apple understood (and, later, so did Bill Gates) that a visual, graphics-based, computer environment would make computing more user-friendly and facilitate the phenomenal growth we have witnessed in the industry. Hence, the birth of the Graphical User Interface, based on icons, pull-down menus, dialog boxes, and the trash can, things people already understood how to use. The same principle applies today to the use of visualization as a marketing tool. Implement techniques and tools such as three dimensions and animation, which people are already familiar with and understand, and they will come.

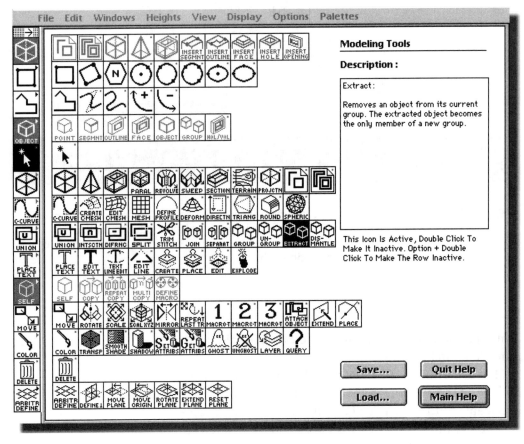

Modeling tool palette from Autodessys' Form Z.
When you select a tool, it gives a description in the box in the upper right hand corner.

Software

Visualization software is described as any application that can perform any combination of modeling, rendering, and/or animation tasks.

Traditional CAD software developers like Autodesk and Intergraph/Bentley Systems have recognized the importance of computer-aided visualization applications and have started including visualization capabilities in their existing CAD applications.

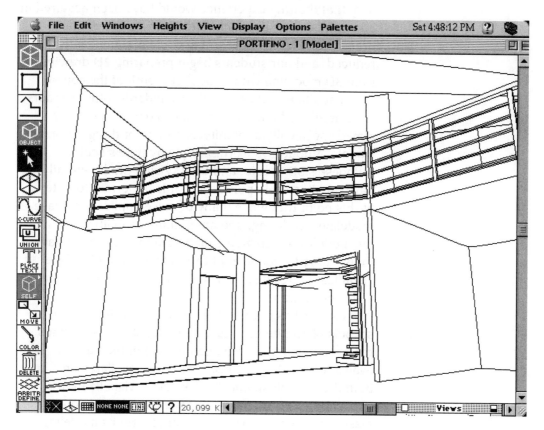

An example of a 3D model created in Form Z.

Both MicroStation and AutoCAD offer add-on modules for creating complex architectural forms as well as some rendering and animation capabilities. The advantage of this approach is that the drafting tools and interface are already familiar, and the learning curve for becoming productive with the modeling module will be significantly reduced.

Case in point: At the University of Miami School of Architecture, everyone must have had drafting experience before taking the 3D visualization course offered. Invariably that drafting experience would have been acquired in an earlier course in which AutoCAD was the primary drafting software. The learning curve is significantly reduced, and our students begin preparing 2D drawings from 3D modeling within the first month of the course.

In addition to these familiar standards, other vendors have developed remarkable stand-alone applications aimed specifically at architects and other design professionals. Autodessys' Form Z, Byte by Byte's Sculpt, Autodesk's 3D Studio, and StrataVision Studio Pro all have architectural applications. It is important to note at this point that while many of these applications have modeling, rendering, and animation capabilities, not all the modules are created equal; therefore, you may have to use more than one application to achieve high-level visualization results. This is also true of the add-ons to CAD applications.

Form Z has become the choice of architects and schools of architecture as a pure modeler. It is perhaps the most comprehensive and intuitive in the pack of available modeling applications and is available on both the Macintosh and PC. Like other visualization applications, Form Z is no snap to learn but, if you master it, there will be no geometric form its modeling tools and your abilities and imagination will not be able to generate.

3-DIMENSIONAL MODELING

Models assist designers and laypersons alike in their journey from design concept to tangible physical form. Within these miniature worlds, we attempt to demonstrate a sense of scale, spatial relationships, human interaction, logistics, and much more. We hope that, after looking at our model, the client will understand and embrace our vision and award us the design commission. With so much riding on the client's perception, it is incumbent upon us to make the best presentation we can, using everything at our disposal.

Technology has provided us with some wonderful tools that can serve to enhance traditional modeling and take our presentations to a whole new level. When compared with cardboard models, 3D computer models offer many advantages.

In terms of design analysis, 3D computer models allow you to market your design ideas to clients by analyzing the scale, form, proportions, circulation flow, and structure of past and present projects from an infinite number of vantage points. Once the model is completed, we can effortlessly set up perspective views and quickly overlay bumwah to create watercolor or color pencil storyboard presentations that can inform clients like no other traditional form of marketing presentation.

Marketing with 3D computer-generated models is more than having access to an infinite amount of perspective views. If you have the right computer-aided design package, the 3D computer models can be the foundation and generator of all the information that you and your clients need to make the appropriate design decisions.

Your firm or employees have probably been using some form of computer-aided design drafting application (CADD) for the past 5 to 10 years but, if all you've been doing is drafting, you have been severely underusing the potential of your favorite tool. When you think about it, 5 or 10 years ago, you were sold a drafting tool. Do you keep an automobile for more than 10 years? Probably not. Every year the manufacturer makes a new model; after 5 years, it's outdated; after 10 years, you would have to visit a junkyard to find spare parts. Why should you treat your CAD application any differently? Some of you are using AutoCAD release 5. Some of you purchased AutoCAD 10 years ago and religiously upgraded each year (driving the same old car, but adding new tires and a paint job annually). We are so busy meeting deadlines, we have not taken the time to analyze the tools that allow us to make these deadlines. In order to market proactively, we may have to leave our comfort zone, break with tradition, and investigate new technologies. Stop driving that clunker and traverse a more efficient route.

Toward an Integrated Solution

Early CAD developers automated the one part of the architectural process (initial design, presentation, development, drafting, cost estimation) that seemed the easiest to automate—drafting. This is still the approach taken by many applications and used by the majority of offices. The drawback to this approach is that by limiting the use of computers to a partial task, such as drafting (and in some cases a separate application for estimating), it does not take full advantage of the awesome power afforded by today's computers. Further, by just addressing one task at a time, the rest of the tasks require the designers to start from scratch each time a new phase of the work is entered.

Thus, there is no way that the design could be used to generate construction documents, or that the construction documents could be used to generate perspective views, and so on. By separating the different phases, unnecessary duplications of work are unavoidable, especially if

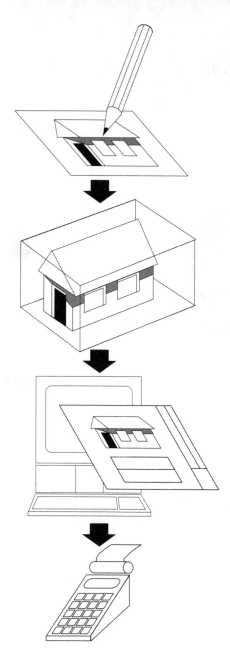

Step 1

In traditional practice, initial massing and design studies are made with pencil. These sketches are then refined and shown to clients for input.

Step 2

Design is translated into either scale models or artist's renderings for final presentation to clients or to gain financing for a project. Because these models or renderings are made by specialists, they tend to be expensive and bulky.

Step 3

In the construction document, drafters translate sketches into working drawings either by pencil or by 2D CAD systems. Changes made to one view (section, elevation, and so on) need to be drawn manually into all other views because they will not update automatically. Models and renderings need to be changed also.

Step 4

Once the construction document drawings are completed, cost estimates, schedules and energy calculations are either done with the help of calculators or stand-alone dedicated software. In either case, data is entered manually. Changes to the drawings or models will have to be reentered and recalculated.

With 3D solid modeling, architectural software architects have to build intelligent computer-generated models of projects only once. All other aspects of the work are "derived" from this model and . . .

Initial design can be viewed by clients and investors immediately in 3D via virtual walkthroughs and animations as well as photorealistic hard-copy renderings.

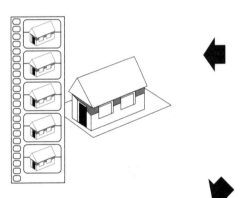

2D construction document drawings are also by-products as they are derived directly from 3D models as sections, elevations, and details.

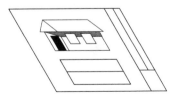

ONCE AND CREATE DERIVATIVES

. . .generated automatically as "by-products": virtual models, renderings and animations, construction drawings, bill-of-materials, marketing and sales materials, ongoing maintenance, and update of plans.

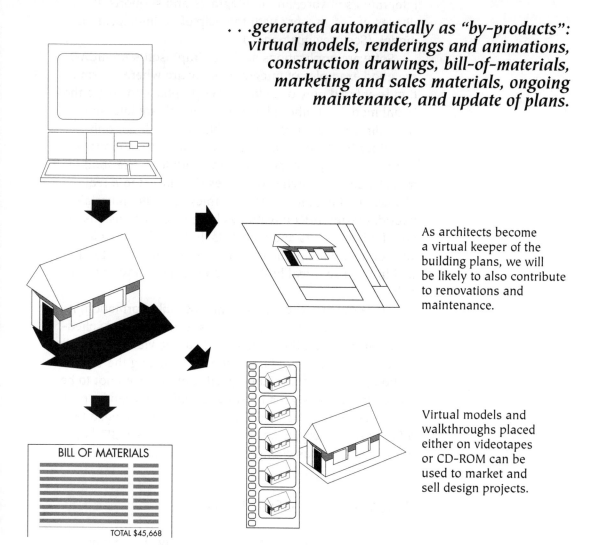

As architects become a virtual keeper of the building plans, we will be likely to also contribute to renovations and maintenance.

Virtual models and walkthroughs placed either on videotapes or CD-ROM can be used to market and sell design projects.

BILL OF MATERIALS

TOTAL $45,668

Bill-of-materials or energy calculations can be made on the fly *during* the design process and not as an afterthought.

the project goes through a great number of revisions. Clearly, there has to be a better way for software to support architectural design work. And there is. It's called integrated software, and it integrates and supports all phases of design work with the help of an intelligent 3D model. (See previous pages.)

Software applications such as Graphisoft's ArchiCAD are good examples of integrated software where information is entered only once in the design phase to create the initial model; all other phases of the work are later derived directly from this model. This approach not only simplifies the task at hand, it represents a revolutionary change in the typical architectural workflow. The solid model created in ArchiCAD comes the closest to a real physical building: its walls have thickness and materials (wood, plaster, brick); windows have three dimensions, as do all other objects and materials. In fact, if you cut a slice of the building, the cut surfaces reveal the materials within just like a real building would appear if we cut it in half.

Since the model contains real material information, it can easily deliver material lists, cost estimates and schedules. Furthermore, the same model can be viewed from all directions and rendered in perspective, making the visualization process a snap. Energy calculations need not to be made after the design is finished; calculations can be part of the design process, and the design can be changed to reflect better energy efficiency. In short, modern 3D-based integrated CAD has changed the way architects work.

PARAMETRIC MODELING

Take a survey of architectural firms in any city, and ask the following question: "Why isn't your firm making use of computer-generated modeling in your design communication and marketing efforts?" I guarantee that the response of the majority of designers would be: "This 3D modeling tool is not fully developed to the point where it can assist my design efforts. I want this tool to be more intuitive, more interactive. My business is designing buildings; I do not want to nor do I have the time to learn these computer modeling software applications. They're not architecturally user-friendly. For example, if I want to build a chair, I should not have to learn modeling to do so. I should be able to provide the computer with information such as style, height, seating and backrest dimensions, expected pressure . . . and as I enter each component, the software application should continually give me the appropriate feedback, allowing me to see changes in real time and complete the design. That is parametric modeling."

Since the advent of CADD, this level of interactive computer design is what architects have been begging for. This is the type of design tool that principals and designers need when they are in meetings with clients. Let's face it, changes are going to be called for in the best of designs. Instead of adjourning to meet the following week, wouldn't it be better to go to your office CADD station and make the necessary changes? Parametric modeling gives us the ability to do what-if scenarios in real time; for example, what would the conference room look like if the ceiling was dropped from 10' to 8'. The key to parametric modeling is real-time interactivity.

Based on our extensive research, the only visualization software application that comes close to this sophisticated level of interactive designing is called Tree Professional, conceived by an architect at Harvard's Graduate School of Design.

Tree Professional is a dedicated, knowledge-based, parametric modeler and this is what differentiates it from all other conventional modelers. With a typical, conventional modeler, you build an object similar to doing cardboard models of your buildings, except that, here, you are working in a computer medium. The conventional modeler does not have any knowledge about the object you are going to model, but it offers you a set of tools for assembling the model piece by piece. Although such modeling may seem intuitive to you because it mimics the way you are used to building your cardboard models, it is often a quite cumbersome and lengthy process, and it requires special skills and lots of time. And, if you do not have a precise knowledge about the object you wish to build, you are lost.

Tree Professional, on the other hand, is a modeler with intelligence; it has the knowledge of objects you wish to build, and it builds them for you. Thus, you do not have to know anything about the anatomy and principles of tree growth, and you can still create a variety of highly photorealistic and biologically accurate trees that will grossly enhance the quality of your presentations.

The process of tree creation is extremely fast because the assemblage of tree elements is done by the computer, not by you.

So, how do you create a tree in Tree Professional? In an episode of *Star Trek, The Next Generation* called "Schisms," the Enterprise is visited by unwelcome aliens who abduct several crew members. The abducted crew members were sedated before being returned to the ship, and they have only vague memories of those experiences. In order to help them recall their memories, Deanna Troi, the ship's counselor, summons them into the Holodeck and, there, they begin to construct the room they all visited by collective memory recollection efforts.

First, they ask the Holodeck to display a desk, and the Holodeck asks for the basic characteristics of the desk such as the size, the height, and the material, and then it displays the desk. From then on, the desk changes incrementally as the crew members, recalling from their memories, supply more details. And, at the end, the object is displayed down to the last minute detail, exactly as remembered by the crew members. The process of assembling this object illustrates very well the idea of parametric modeling.

With Tree Professional, the process of tree creation is similar except, of course, for the differences in the user interface. You start with the default tree or a tree preloaded from the Tree library, and then ask the program to adjust the tree's essential characteristics (parameters) such as the height, the curvature and density of branches, the type and color of leaves, and many more. The changes can be minor, which will result in a slightly different variation of the same tree, or they can be substantial, resulting in a new species. Each parameter adjustment is recorded on the model instantly so that you have full awareness of the changes during the modeling process.

When you export the 3D model, you can ask TREE to adjust the resolution and detail of the tree, which will have profound implications on the size of the model. You have a choice to model the same tree with, for example, as many as a 50,000 polygons and as few or fewer than a thousand polygons. By these adjustments, you can control effectively the polygon size of your scenery by putting less detailed, small models in the background and high-fidelity, larger models in the foreground.

If you own ElectricImage Animation System, you can take advantage of Tree EIAS, a breakthrough product that goes one step further in making good use of the parametric modeling concept, allowing you to model trees in real time directly into the EIAS scene without using the .dxf and .fact files. Thanks to the fact that no data files are generated, the modeling-in and positioning of trees on the scene is practically instantaneous. Furthermore, it takes just a moment to adjust the resolution and detail of your model or to replace it with another tree from the library. And, with the "EI abstract" feature, you can choose to model a tree in much simpler form while positioning it on the scene. The Camera will render it in full detail. Once you experience the speed and versatility of Tree EIAS, as well as the time savings that it brings to your projects, you will never even think of going back to work with the .dxf or .fact files.

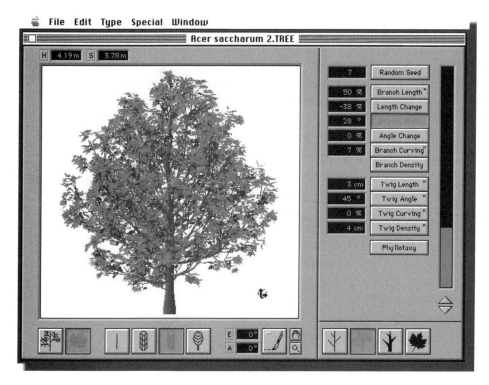

Figure 5.1 Tree Professional's canvas displays a tree preloaded from the Tree library. You change the tree by selecting any of the characteristics (parameters) and adjusting its value with the slider on the right-hand side of the window. As you move the slider, Tree registers the changes and displays the resulting tree.

An integral part of Tree Professional package is a CD with the libraries of parametric files of broadleaf and conifer trees, palms, and bushes—there are over 160 plants in the library. You can use these trees as they are or modify them by changing any of the parameters. In the library you will find red maple, weeping birch, European beech, horse chestnut, apple, Japanese maple, sycamore, poplar, cherry plum, white oak, weeping willow, American elm, linden, sugar maple, ginkgo, spruce, pine, fir, cedar, Guadeloupe palm, coconut palm, fan palm, date palm,

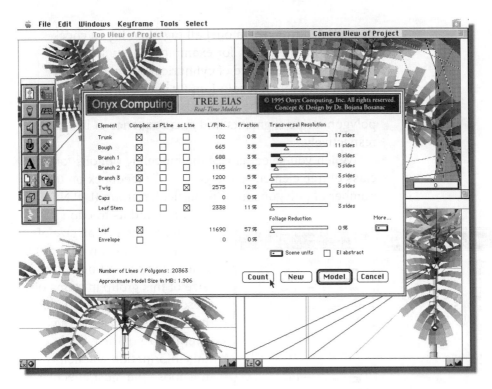

Figure 5.2 By pressing the Tree EIAS icon in the EIAS's Object Palette, you call up the Tree EIAS dialog, which allows you to open any tree created by Tree Professional, adjust the resolution and detail of the selected tree, and model the tree directly into the EIAS scene in the chosen units.

royal palm, cotton palm, and many more.

Tree Professional displays the power of parametric modeling at its best and is giving us a glimpse into the ways future modelers will operate, similar to *Star Trek*'s Holodeck. Looking at the Holodeck, one cannot help but think of it as being the ultimate parametric modeler.

On the far left-hand side of the dialog in Figure 5.2, you can see the Element column, which displays all the classes of principal tree elements. Each class can be modeled at up to three different levels of detail, or it can be excluded from the model all together. If you check Complex for the trunk, for example, the trunk will be modeled as a sequence of cylindrical segments of the chosen transversal resolution. By checking as PLine or as Line, the trunk will be modeled as a sequence of one-polygon stripe segments and as a sequence of lines, respectively.

When you select any of the modeling options for any class of tree elements, you get instant feedback on the number of polygons for this particular group (L/P No. column) and its fraction relative to the overall size of the model (Fraction column). Thus, you see not only the size of this group in terms of absolute polygon numbers, but also its impact on the overall size of the model. And this information will help you to choose the most effective strategy in lowering the number of polygons for a particular tree. Once a tree is on the scene, its detail and resolution can be changed simply by recalling the Tree EIAS dialog and remodeling the tree.

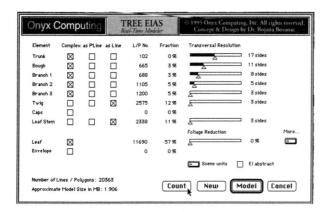

The EI abstract feature is another extra useful time-saver that allows you to move a tree around the scene much more easily than if you were moving the .fact model. With this feature, you can choose to model a tree in an abstracted form (only the trunk and the crown envelope) while you are positioning it on the scene, and later the Camera will render it in full detail. The crown envelope gives you the mass of fully detailed tree, yet it has only 140 polygons no matter how large the tree is. And you can move these 140 polygons around the scene in a fraction of the time it would take you to move around the fully detailed tree.

ANALYTICAL RENDERING

In order to bring a building to life, architects traditionally commission a rendering. The artist interprets the plans, adds real-world building materials, foliage, and people to simulate the real thing. Well, you can do the same things and much more with a 3D computer model. Most rendering applications are accompanied by tons of building materials including brick, glass, carpeting, and marble to name just a few. An entire software sub-industry exists to provide textures of computer renderings for architects and other design professionals. If for some reason you can't find a particular material, you can always scan it and create your own texture. The same techniques used by traditional renderers can be utilized on your computer model. You can adjust parameters including lighting, shadows, opacity, and reflectiveness of various surfaces.

The premise is that you want to show your potential clients your understanding of how the building materials that you have selected will look on the surfaces of the proposed three-dimensional form. As designers, our job is to create beautiful functional forms and spaces that manifest themselves into architecture. However, rendering applications such as Autodesk's 3D Studio presents us with a communication tool to create much more than beautiful images. They give us the opportunity to market design services much more effectively, by communicating to potential clients the building's analytical features such as horizontal and vertical circulation, volume, structure, massing, as well as building-site relationship.

In the following section we will show you how to set up a computer-generated model in 3D Studio using cameras, lighting, materials, and composition. In addition, you will see how two projects are presented and analyzed using the visualization tools of 3D Studio.

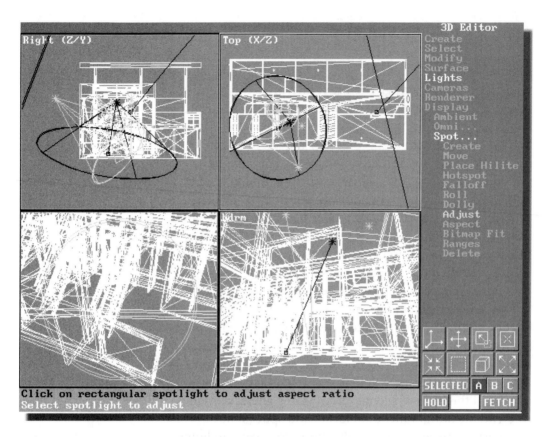

Lighting, composition (camera setup), and form are the most important elements when using rendering as a design analytical communication tool. Once a three-dimensional model is imported into a visualization application like Autodesk's 3D Studio, you first begin adding lighting to your scene. Basically, there are three types of lighting: ambient, omni (used to accent surfaces), and spot.

Ambient Light

In 3D Studio, this type of lighting simulates bounced light that fills a room or environment.

Omni Light

In 3D Studio, this type of lighting has point light sources that accent surfaces of a structure or act as a fill light source.

Spot Light

In 3D Studio, this type of lighting is the primary light source for exterior renderings, like the sun.

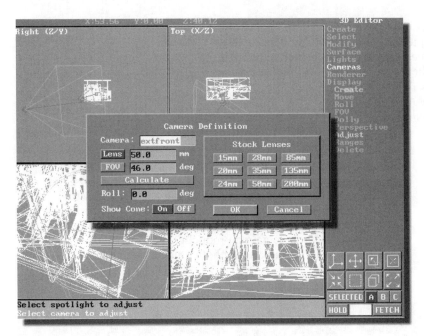

By activating the camera dialog, you are on your way to selecting the appropriate camera that would define perspective views.

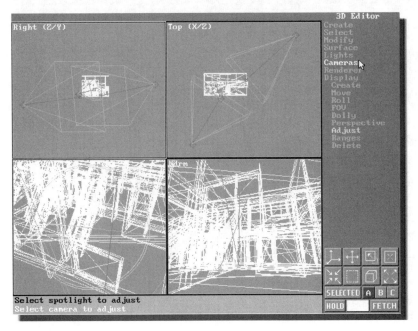

Cameras placed in the right and top views of your three-dimensional model can be communicated and analyzed in the resulting perspective view windows.

Below: As architects, we may not understand many of the ever changing computer terminologies that continually infiltrate our practice. However, the selection of building materials and finishes is an integral part of our everyday duties as designers. From within 3D Studio Max this is where the library of materials such as brick, stucco, glass, tile, and more are selected.

Top right: Once selected, the materials are edited and saved to be mapped onto the appropriate layers of your computer-generated model. As the graphic shows, the Material Editor also gives you the ability to view the selected materials. The Material Editor is like an artist's palette. Although it may look quite intimidating, it is really very simple to gain a productive working knowledge of this tool in order to create photorealistic renderings.

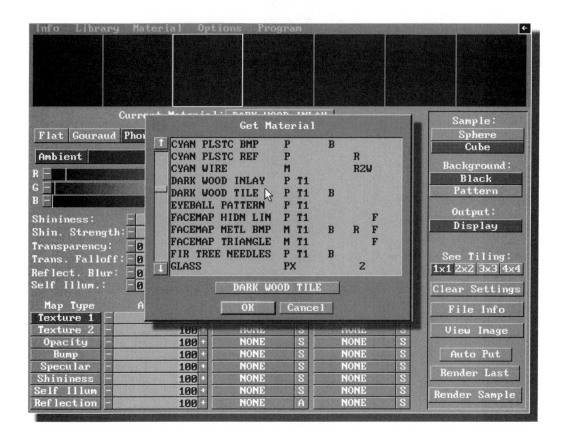

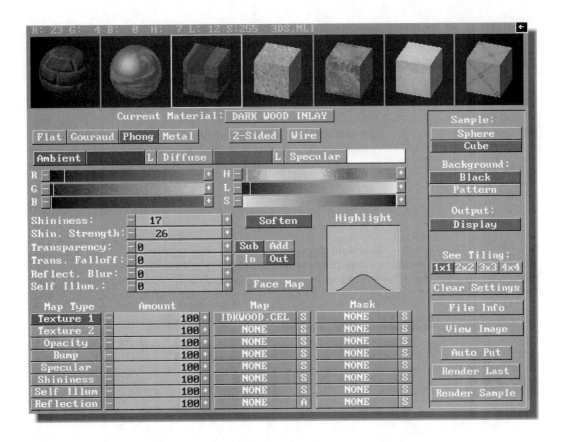

Instead of lecturing to you on how rendering can be used as an analytical tool during your marketing efforts, we thought that it would be best to show you how this can be accomplished. The following examples are a series of computer-generated models that were created using Autodessys' Form Z and Autodesk's AutoCAD. All analytical renderings were created using Autodesk's 3D Studio. With the appropriate training and practice, we can all create pretty Hollywood-style renderings. If that is your sole intent, you would be vastly underusing the technology of your computer, as well as the visualization software application. The challenge that we present here is to take this technology to the edge: do design analysis, and communicate to your clients elements of your designs that are impossible to show with chipboard or traditional models. Break all the rules. Apply a material of glass to the entire building, so you can analyze form, structure, and spaces that may be hidden. Create renderings that explode the model to analyze and communicate building assembly.

This dialog displays all of the layers that represent individual elements that make up your computer-generated model. The materials and finishes selected from the Material Editor would be applied to each layer.

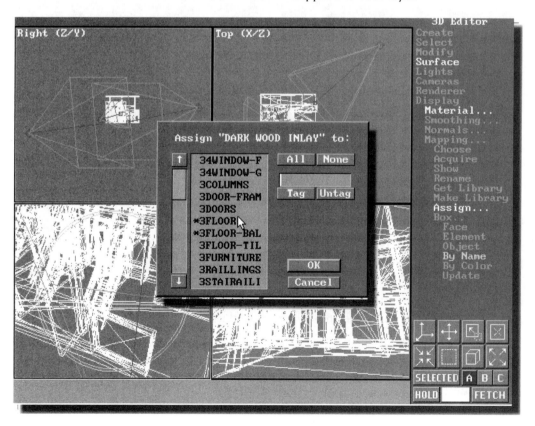

Here, solids and voids are successfully communicated by applying glass and an opaque material to the building's surfaces. Also, for maximum exposure, the same building is shown at two different angles.

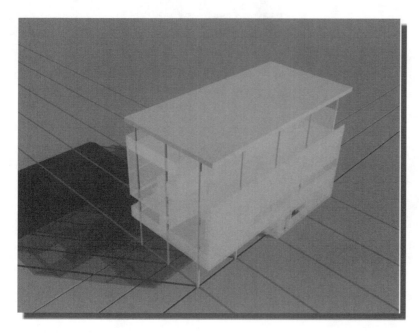

Here, glass is applied to the non-structural elements of the building, and an opaque material is applied to illustrate all vertical and horizontal structures. A grid is carved in the ground to further emphasize the building's structure.

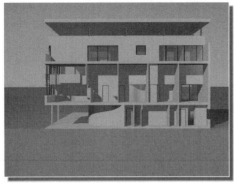

Below and right: Another technique for analyzing interior spaces of a multi-structure building is to extrude each floor plan so one can understand the chronology of stacking each floor.
In this illustration, the lowest level of the building is shown to your left, while the uppermost level is to your right.

Above: Slice the building in your CADD or modeling software application, import the section into a rendering application where you can adjust cameras and lighting to assist in your analysis of interior spaces.

Below: A finished rendering that shows the building fully assembled.

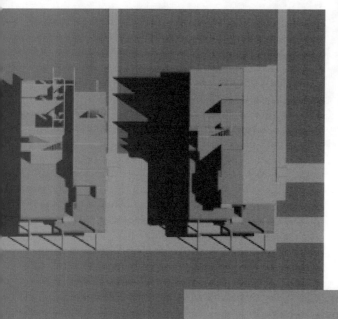

Above: Here, the rendered section is used to analyze the height relationships of interior spaces.

Below: A finished rendering that shows the building fully assembled.

Do not be afraid
to hide layers,
in order to show
key spatial
relationships.

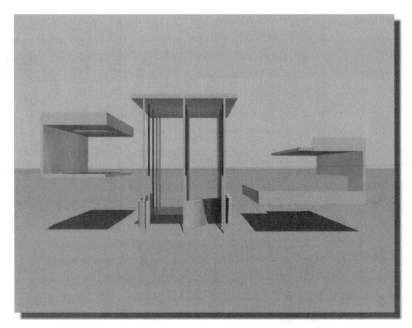

Very clever tech-
nique here, show-
ing horizontal
members in glass
in concert with the
finished rendering.
Great marketing
communication
technique for
clients who need
to understand
your design.

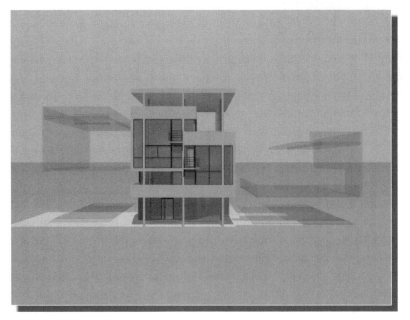

By adjusting the camera to match an isometric view, you can communicate a building's interior spaces as well as show how it would be stacked all in one view.

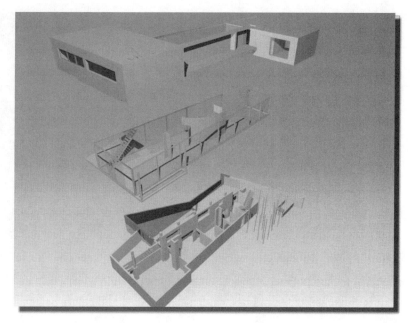

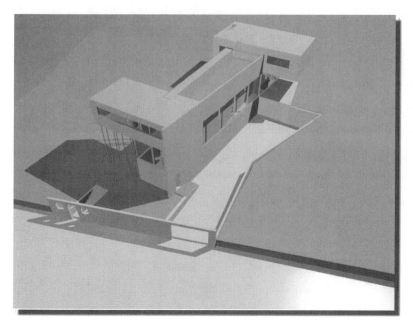

If you illustrate the building's assembly as shown here, be sure to tie it back to a rendering of the building fully assembled. Remember you are marketing to a community that wants to understand the parts as well as the whole.

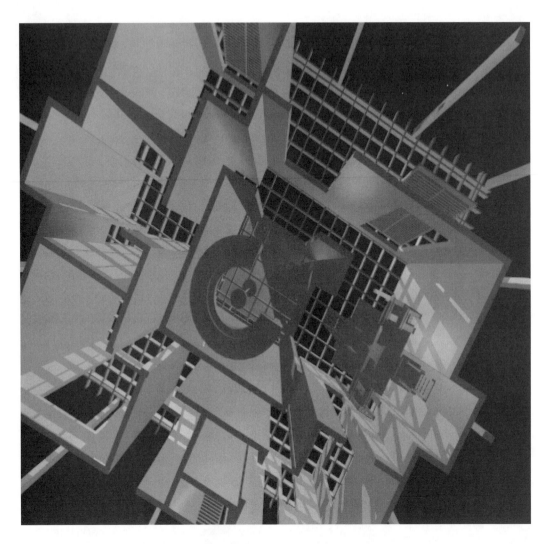

Understanding photography would definitely assist you in creating analytically rendered views such as this one. Here, the camera tool in 3D Studio was manipulated to create this perspective view looking from the ground up into the building's envelope.

Here *(left and below)* are two very dramatic and effective demonstrations of how computer rendering can be used as an effective analytical and persuasive marketing device. These are great examples of pushing this visualization technology to its limits. In addition, these types of analytical images cannot be achieved through chipboard modeling nor traditional renderings.

This view was created by applying glass and wire to the surfaces of this building, for detailed structural analysis.

Two years ago, I was in a meeting with one of my clients and the interior design firm. This was during the design development stage and we were making a computer visualization presentation of what the building would look like completed. To my amazement, the client who had major difficulty understanding the construction document drawings was more interested in the assembly of the building—the construction phasing. This does not

Using the suite of rendering tools in 3D Studio, this marketing image was created to show the building's assembly.

mean that he was not impressed with the vision of his finished building. To the contrary, the multimedia marketing presentation was a blockbuster. This was a client who had very fiscally conservative partners who understood construction. As a result, we were then charged with altering our presentation to show the building's assembly. We used the same rendering tools that were applied to the slick marketing presentation to show how the building would be assembled.

Here, a view from above shows how the exploded members of the rendered computer model would be assembled.

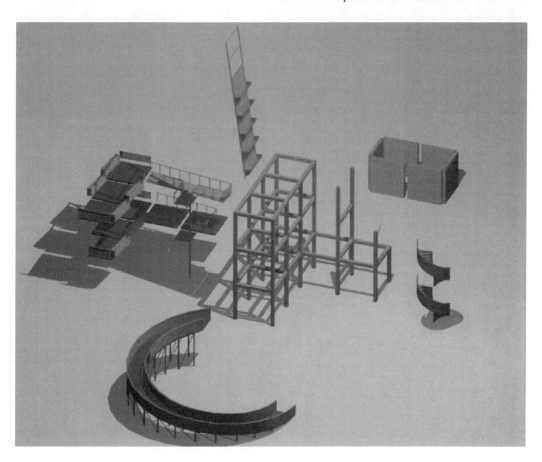

POST-RENDERING EDITING

Since I have been writing, teaching, and consulting about computer-generated imaging, I have been constantly told by colleagues that the resulting images from rendering software appear very unreal and cold. This is probably because, as

architects, our visual design representations have always had an artistic, inviting appearance. As a result, many frustrated architects stayed away from rendering software. That is, until post-rendering editing applications like Adobe Photoshop became available. This group of software applications is based on extensions known as filters.

Filters in image editing software applications provide you with one of the easiest and quickest means of creating visually exciting results, once applied to your computer-generated renderings. The filters that are shipped with Adobe Photoshop allow you to enhance your marketing graphics with artistic effects such as impressionistic, mosaic, and emboss, to name a few. Photoshop, which is available on both Macintosh and PC plat-

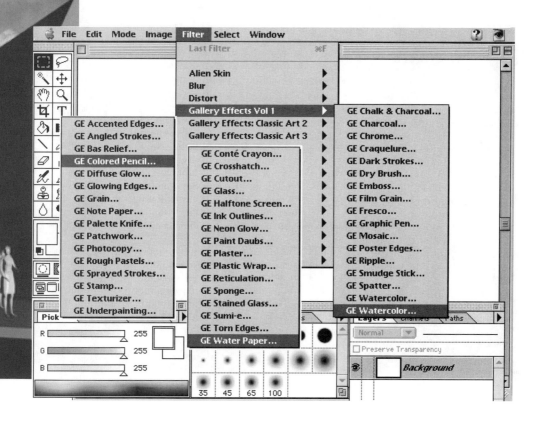

forms, also supports plug-in filters such as pastel, oil paint, watercolor, charcoal, and graphic pen developed in supporting packages like Adobe's Gallery Effects series of Classical Art filters. Consequently, from a single rendering we can use lighting and artistic filters to create additional marketing images limited only by our imaginations.

But we also have to convincingly market our design ideas to current as well as potential clients. The possibilities presented to us via computer technology are just additional design tools.

The ability to use the plug-in filter feature of an image-editing software application like Adobe Photoshop can be an architect's best friend. Once you have completed a computer-generated rendering, that file can be then imported into Photoshop, where you can access a variety of filters to achieve the appropriate artistic effect.

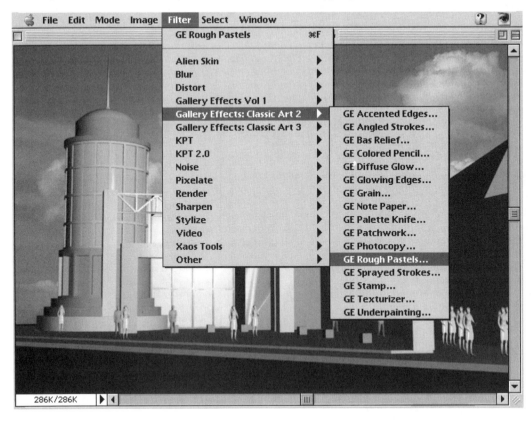

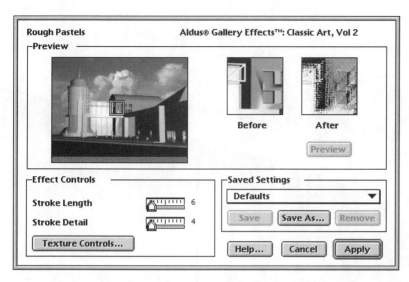

In this example, a rough pastel filter from Adobe Gallery Effects set of Classical Art is being applied to the rendering. Like a paintbrush, these plug-in filters give you control over stroke length, stroke detail, and texture. You can experiment on a small portion of the image before applying the desired artistic effect to the entire rendering.

In addition to artistic plug-in filters, Adobe Photoshop is packed with lighting effect filters that allow further manipulation of your marketing graphics. A rending that was poorly lighted in your rendering software application can be given new life from within Photoshop's editing studio.

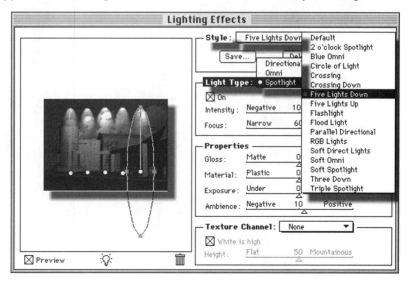

GET
PLUGGED-IN

MARKETING WITH ANIMATION

Thanks to Walt Disney, most of us understand what animation is and how it works, be it computer or hand-drawn. An animation is a series of still frames that, when displayed at a speed of about 30 frames per second, simulates motion. Disney's cartoonists are some of the best in the world at creating hand-drawn animations but, today, even they are making use of computer technology in the creation of some of their biggest hits. In *Beauty and the Beast*, portions of the movie were created with computer animation and, their latest production, *Toy Story* (in conjunction with a company called Pixar), was created from start to finish using computer animation.

Animation for architects makes use of the computer-generated model and the computer's processing power to create animation walk-throughs, which can greatly enhance a client's understanding and speed up the approval process. You start by defining a path through the model for a camera to follow, take pictures and render the frames. The more pictures you render, the smoother the animation.

ElectricImage Animation is one software application that can be invaluable to your marketing efforts. It is currently the fastest software-based renderer available on the personal computer, able to render tall buildings in a single bound! (Okay, so I got a little carried away!) It can, however, render an animation three to four times faster than other similar applications and can therefore keep pace with an ever-changing design process. Within the last two years, we have written two books and nine articles for all of the major architecture publications and, in the process, had the opportunity to evaluate many rendering and animation applications. In all of our evaluations on both the Macintosh and Intel-based platforms, ElectricImage was the fastest.

We asked ourselves why there was such a vast difference in performance if there was a common platform. The answer was, and still is, superior engineering, a concept we can all appreciate.

Scenario: You have a client in your office for a 10:00 A.M. meeting. He likes most of what he sees but won't sign off until you make certain changes. He won't be able to meet with you until next week, so, if you don't get a signature today, the project will probably be delayed.

Solution: Have your designers make the necessary changes while you take your client out to lunch. Use ElectricImage Animation to rerender the changes to the model. You return from lunch, the changes are made, the client approves, the project moves ahead, on schedule. Your client will not only love you and use you again, but will also recommend you to colleagues.

Case Study

C4 Studio was hired by the South Beach Citizen Coalition as a consultant to conduct visualization studies in an effort to assist urban designers from Urbaniza Architecture and Planning, Miami, to show the impact that a 75-foot-high condo development would have on the fabric of a two-story neighborhood. During a period of three weeks, we had several working meetings and charettes with the architect, urban planners, citizen coalition, and city commission in an effort to present our recommendations.

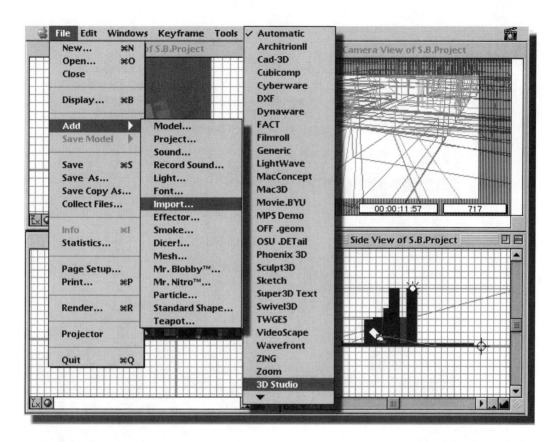

Step 1

The computer model was generated with Autodessys' Form Z, and then imported into Autodesk 3D Studio for analytical evaluations of the proposed design. Because our services included several working sessions, charettes and city commission presentations, we needed the ability to make changes to the animations and show results quickly. As a result, we took advantage of ElectricImage's (EI) ability to import a large variety of file formats, and imported the 3D Studio file into this application for lightning-speed animations.

Step 2

Next, after developing a storyboard, we set out to create several animation sequences. For this, the Keyframe dialog was activated. From the top
or plan view, cameras were placed along a desired path. In the diagram,
each camera represents a keyframe. ElectricImage then generated the
animation sequence by interpolating between each keyframe.

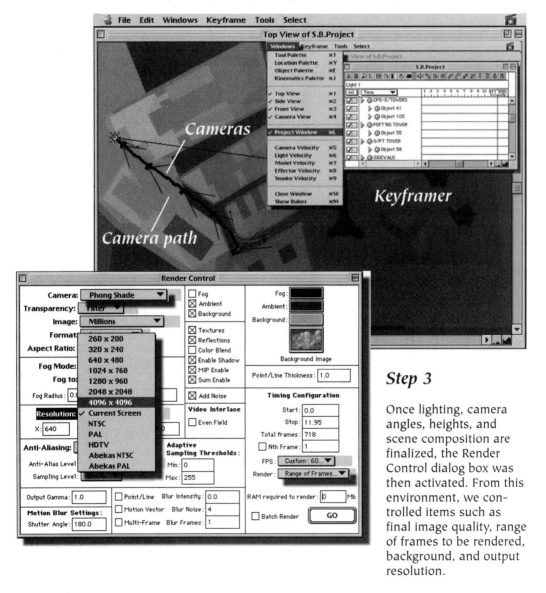

Step 3

Once lighting, camera
angles, heights, and
scene composition are
finalized, the Render
Control dialog box was
then activated. From this
environment, we con-
trolled items such as
final image quality, range
of frames to be rendered,
background, and output
resolution.

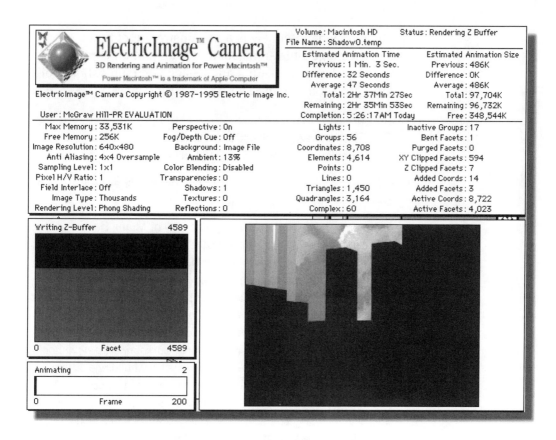

Step 4

This camera dialog box was indispensable to us during the meeting and charettes. The progress window provided us, the urban designers and client, with real-time feedback that facilitated instantaneous design evaluation. Other important information that allowed us to manage the animation included estimated animation time, estimated animation size, and memory usage.

The following interview is a demonstration of how ElectricImage's real-time computer animation capabilities were used as a marketing and design communication tool for a project in Miami, Florida.

CC: Curtis Charles
GD: Gladys Diaz, Architect and Owner,
    Urbaniza Architecture and Planning

CC: Give us a brief explanation of the project that we worked on and then I'll move onto the questions.

GD: Okay. Our firm was hired by the city of Miami Beach to consult on a transaction that was already in progress. The project was proposed by a private sector developer to take a piece of property that he had an option on, and sell it to the city. In exchange for giving them favorable pricing, he wanted to be able to transfer 400,000 square feet of air rights to another site while upzoning that other site to a high-rise. These waterfront properties, which had very high zoning, surrounded a neighborhood that had mostly two- and three-story buildings. There was a great deal of protest by the citizens of the community who did not want buildings in that area built so high. We were asked by the city to evaluate the physical as well as the financial proposal that was offered by the developer.

CC: As far as the physical proposal, one of the things you did was hire C4 Studio to do the computer visualization. What was the thinking behind that?

GD: To help the commissioners and the citizens of the community, who by nature don't think in three-dimensions but who are accustomed to very high-tech images on television and the media. We felt we had to have a quality that would grab the attention of the viewer and communicate the fact that this was a very dense site, and that if we transferred the 400,000 square feet, there would be a substantial amount of building, and a serious problem could occur because of this proposed density. The only way we could do that was to provide computer imaging that would communicate quickly and readily what we couldn't communicate in two-dimensional form.

CC: So how did the computer model and animation assist in achieving that?

GD: It was the single most powerful tool that we had in our presentation because it communicated in three-dimensional form the potential dangers of the proposed project; it forced negotiation. They asked us to continue working on the project and to assist the city in developing urban design guidelines. It also caused the city to freeze its negotiations subject to our team assisting the developer and the city of Miami Beach staff to develop urban design guidelines that would mitigate the damage caused by this project.

CC: Would you say that it was the single entity that communicated the idea? Couldn't this have been done in traditional 2D?

GD: Not really. Remember, society, the general public, is accustomed to computer images and three-dimensional images. So when you have a drawing that is just a 2D projection, it's very hard for the general public to understand because it requires a certain degree of imagination. If you give the public the information that they can readily digest, that quantum leap of the imagination does not have to occur.

CC: Would you say that, in terms of the ideas you had, this was a good use as a marketing tool?

GD: Absolutely. It's not just a marketing tool; it's really a technical service. It's not just to promote a concept—it's gone beyond that; it was actually an intrinsic part of the presentation to the public. It was an analytical tool.

CC: What about the meetings you had with the community groups and the city; how was this tool used as a communication device?

GD: It enabled us to show the citizens what we were thinking, why the issues we were pointing out were key. We also had an on-line setup during the community planning workshop where we could input the data right then and there, and the citizens saw that it was very interactive, that they participated in the process. That was very important.

CC: So, you made changes in real time?

GD: Exactly. It makes the community part of the process.

CC: As you look back on this experience, how do you think your firm is going to use it in the future, and what do you say to other firms thinking of using it as a design tool?

GD: If it's affordable—most of these public projects have limited budgets—I think it should be done in every project. I think that is key, and I think we are going to continue to use it as much as we can. I'm encouraging all the students I work with to study animation as part of their technical training program because they need to understand how this can be part of their practice.

CC: Do you think that the presentations really swayed the city?

GD: Swayed is not the word; it pushed them over the edge. This computer image showed them graphically exactly what could happen. It showed graphically how the heights could cause a problem, how the shadows that were going to be cast by these taller buildings were going to be a problem. The streetscape, however, was not as useful as the shadow study because it didn't have as much information.

CC: How important was the shadow study?

GD: It was the most important.

CC: What did the shadow study show them?

GD: That the building would create shadows during the summer months over the entire park, which is a public park; and in the winter months, it would keep the beach completely in shadow the entire afternoon. It made them suddenly realize that all these public facilities would be completely in shadow, and that was a problem since people come to Miami Beach to use the public facilities and be in the sun.

THE BENEFITS OF COMPUTER VISUALIZATION

Scale

For obvious reasons, it is impossible to build a full-scale cardboard model. Some architects may attempt to do full-scale break-outs of portions of the model to give a client a sense of scale, but this can be expensive and time-consuming. Even so, many contemporary architects do build full-scale portions of a structure in order to give the client some sense of human scale. On the other hand, consider a computer model. With a computer model, as with CAD, you build in full-scale or real-world units. A 10-foot wall is entered as 10 feet on the computer model. You can then display whichever portion of the model you want by placing a camera anywhere in the model you choose: inside the building, up on the rafters, even overhead for a helicopter-like view. You and your client will have the opportunity to explore the proposed design from an infinite number of vantage points.

Detail

With the approach to scale just mentioned, you can take a close look at details included in the model without having to do a separate detail model or use a magnifying glass. You simply place the camera directly in front of the portion of the model that is of interest to you and, in effect, take a snapshot.

"God is in the detail."
—Ludwig Mies Van Der Rohe

Time

Even though both computer models and cardboard models have the same starting points—blueprints or CAD files—it takes considerably more time and effort to build a cardboard model. This is because the computer automates many of the time-consuming tasks involved in building a model; 3D computer models can be built directly from your CAD files.

You can save your CAD file as a .dxf file and bring it into your modeling program. Using a modeling technique called extrusion, you can build the walls right from the DXF plan. Even with the use of expensive laser technology, which cuts the pieces of the model using information contained in the CAD file, cardboard models cannot compare with computer models with respect to speed.

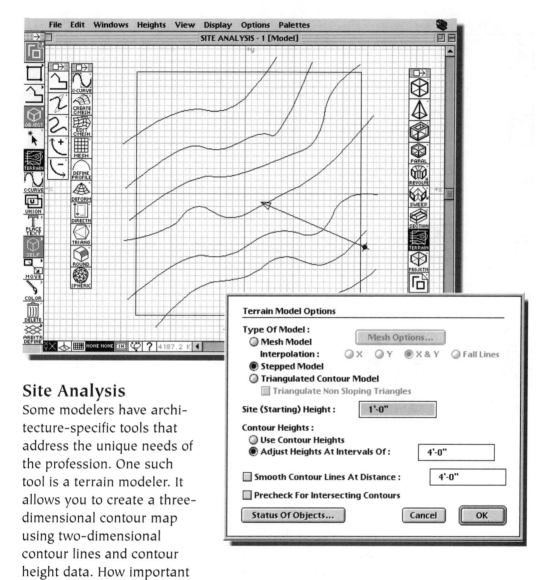

Site Analysis

Some modelers have architecture-specific tools that address the unique needs of the profession. One such tool is a terrain modeler. It allows you to create a three-dimensional contour map using two-dimensional contour lines and contour height data. How important is this modeling design tool? Well, when was the last time your firm was short-listed for a design commission, and you presented your design proposal in absence of site study diagrams or a foam-core model with a structure stuck somewhere on the site?

The client needs to know that we understand the site before you create appropriate design solutions based on a

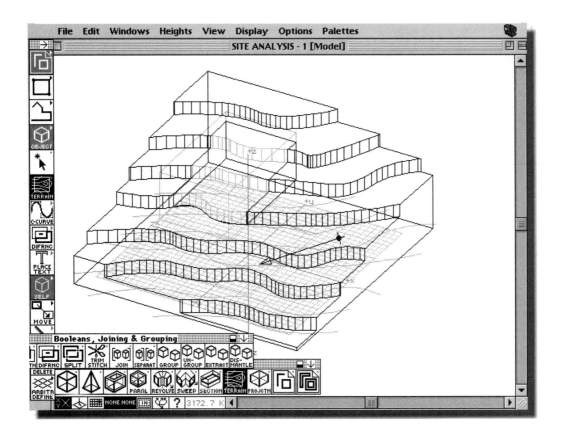

careful analysis of the site features. In addition, unless you practice in Florida, you know that a great challenge to many designers is that of placing a building on a sloping or heavily contoured site. In order to communicate your design solution to clients, you would probably have to build several foam-core site models illustrating cuts and fills. A modeling software such as Autodessys' Form Z automates this tedious design task.

Sun Analysis

The impact of the sun is a critically important design consideration. You can conduct sun studies on your computer model for any geographical location, any day of the year, any time of the day. Computer visualization applications animate the path of the sun for the parameters you define, and automatically generate the shadows appropriate for the time and location. This design tool gives you all the information you need to make informed responsive design decisions. What a marvelous tool!

Real-Time Interactivity

With respect to interactivity, again it's no contest. Three-dimensional software's ability to serve as a real-time visualization tool brings up the next important marketing factor, where the 3D modeling software has a definite edge over other CAD software and traditional model making—it can allow the architect to interact with the client and make important design decisions in real time. The client can sit next to the architect and experience the design as a 3D walk-through, thus the chance for mis-communication is dramatically reduced thereby saving cost and time for the client. Because of this saving, as well as the "whiz-bang" effect of being able to "tour" a yet-to-be-built project, clients are apt to seek out architects who can provide them with this technology.

You can respond to what-if scenarios in a way that is simply impossible with a cardboard model. You can make design changes and immediately see and understand the implications of that change. You can experiment freely with different forms and configurations, confident in your knowledge of the outcome. Explore your project from every imaginable angle. Answer questions such as "I wonder what this atrium would look like from over here." Your clients will appreciate your responsiveness to their questions and concerns regarding their project.

EMERGING INNOVATIONS IN VISUALIZATION

Sometimes the client needs to present the project to others; for instance, to obtain financing or approval from local or federal authorities. As the client's need to market increases, so will his or her need to get the best possible marketing presentation.

Apple Computer has developed a virtual reality technology called QuickTime VR that allows Macintosh and Windows users to experience spatial interactions using only a personal computer with a mouse or trackball and keyboard. No special hardware or accessories are needed. QuickTime VR (QTVR) uses an innovative 360-degree panoramic photography technique that enables VR-like experiences of real-world spaces and objects.

On every architectural project, the proposed site is carefully studied for contextual purposes. We want to convey to the client that we understand all of the site's assets as well as challenges. Traditionally, architects use chipboard site models or photography in these marketing presentations. We achieve the latter by standing across the street of the proposed site and taking photographs of a streetscape. The photographs are then glued together to create a 180-degree view of the site. Used as a backdrop, proposed design solutions are then sketched on overlays. With QuickTime VR, these same photographic prints can be scanned into the computer. Once scanned, you can use QTVR's electronic stitching tool to seamlessly "stitch" the photographs to create a panoramic image. After compression and distortion correction, the MakeSingleNodeMovie command creates a QuickTime VR

To photograph a QuickTime VR scene, you have to put a 35mm camera with a 15mm lens on a tripod and shoot a series of pictures, turning the camera 30 degrees after each exposure. The photographs are then developed and digitized onto a photo CD.

As discussed, QuickTime can be used to piece together photographs to make a panorama.

To solve distortion problems, QuickTime VR warps the images. Then it automatically maps the overlapping features and stitches the images together. This warping can, however, create some distortion of its own.

When you open a scene, the QuickTime VR Player corrects the
distortion in the part of the image displayed by the Player window.
As you navigate, the software keeps up with your movements,
correcting and displaying your view of the panorama "on the fly."

panoramic movie. The panoramic movie allows architects
to explore and experience the site as never before. The
architect and client can "walk" into and around the site,
analyzing the context. This is an impressive medium with
which to convey your understanding of site and urban
issues to potential clients.

QTVR also allows you to create scenes based on a
sequence of images generated from your computer-generated 3D model. It is not limited only to photographs of real
sites. You begin by importing your model into your favorite
rendering application, and setting up electronic cameras to
take the required series of snapshots of the area in question. Then, following the process just described, you can
use QTVR to create an interactive panoramic movie of your
3D model. This gives you and your clients the opportunity
to have a VR experience of proposed projects long before
any earth is turned or the first brick is laid.

Although Apple's Authoring Tool presents a viable
solution for creating interactive real-time QuickTime VR
movies, its execution requires some knowledge of computer
programming. Fortunately for us, several software develop-

ers have begun to integrate the creation of VR movies into their 3D applications somewhat like 3D modeling is integrated into CAD applications. Such is the case with Graphisoft's ArchiCAD. It has created a QuickTime VR plug-in that works within ArchiCAD to create panoramic navigable movies. It simplifies the process considerably.

Graphisoft ArchiCAD's solution is based on a QuickTime VR (system) extension that works with Apple Macintosh, Power Macintosh, Windows, and Windows NT platforms. However, Windows-based ArchiCAD users must have access to a Macintosh to create VR scenes, but they can still save and view their ArchiCAD projects on their Windows-based PCs equipped with QuickTime and the QuickTime VR Player.

Architecture and design/build firms would love to have this powerful tool to communicate with clients, potential home buyers, prospective tenants, and almost anyone with a desktop computer equipped with QuickTime 2 + . For example, in the case of a housing development, for a design/build firm, it would be more economically feasible to create QuickTime VR panoramic movies of all the building types, distribute them to potential buyers on diskettes or CD-ROMs, who could in real time, with the use of a PC and mouse, "walk through" each room, in whatever order desired, than to physically construct model homes. With this technology, you can offer your clients a completely rendered 3D environment that they can explore freely, simply by moving a mouse. It is important to note here that prior to Apple's introduction of this technology, architects were unable to avail themselves of this opportunity without a significant outlay of cash for special hardware. Apple's QuickTime VR brings virtual reality to all of us.

This solution developed by Apple and embraced by Graphisoft for developing VR movies does two things for potential clients. First, it gives them a sense of being a participant, literally by taking control of the mouse to explore their future offices or homes. Second, it gives

CREATING QUICKTIME VR MOVIES WITH ARCHICAD

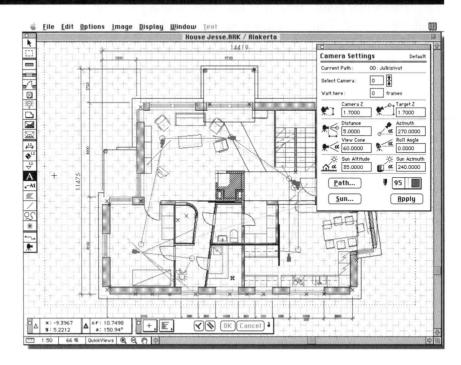

Step 1

Activate the camera settings and set the camera height, target height, cone of vision, and sun altitude. From the plan projection view, place cameras.

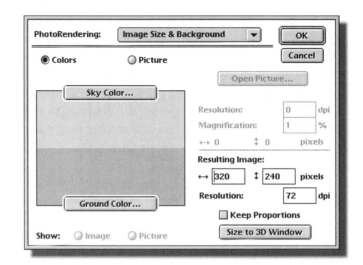

Step 2

In order to set the final size of the navigable QuickTime movie, activate the PhotoRendering dialog.

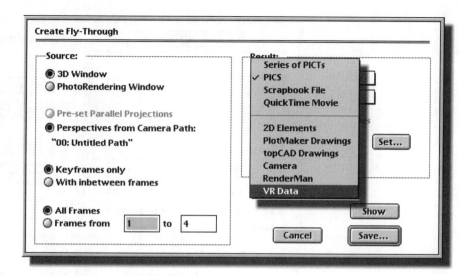

Step 3

Go to Create Fly-Through dialog,
select VR Data for results, and
enter the settings as shown.

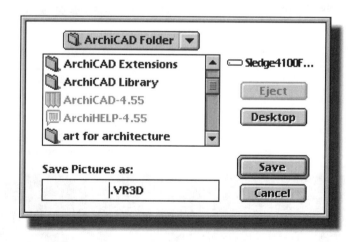

Step 4

The program will save a file
with the extension VR3D.
When completed, quit
ArchiCAD, and double-click
on this file's icon to launch
the VR Maker.

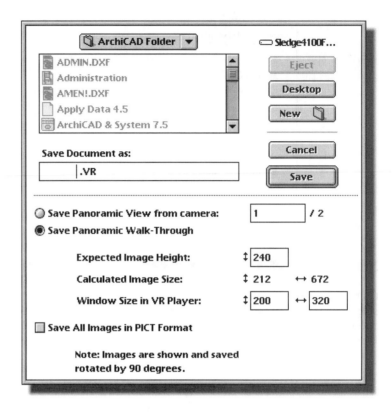

Step 5

Give the movie a name, then click OK and the program will start to generate the VR movie.

Step 6

This is the resulting 360-degree panoramic strip, which, once opened in the Movie Player, becomes navigable.

Step 7

This is what the final navigable QuickTime VR movie looks like from within the Movie Player. This movie can be played back from any Apple or Intel-based computer.

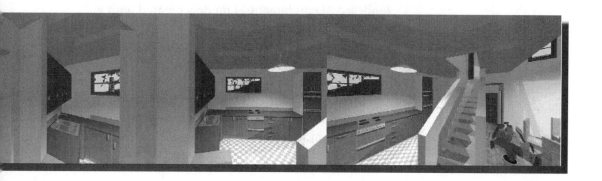

them a good feel for how things will work in three dimensions. Without this kind of visualization, many clients don't understand what the builder or architect is presenting. QuickTime Virtual Reality technology enables clients to be at ease with their design and make informed decisions, earlier, thus saving time and money.

Virtual Reality Modeling Language (VRML)

VRML is a developing standard for describing interactive three-dimensional virtual worlds delivered across the Internet. It is an open, platform-independent file format (like DXF) for 3D graphics on the Internet.

The 3D architectural model that you created for that design presentation can now be uploaded onto the Internet where you and potential clients can virtually walk through the model of the building, analyze issues such as circulation flow, physical spaces, study details and views, test finishes, and building materials under varying lighting conditions. With VRML, you, your potential clients, and consultants, all of whom can be in different geographical locations across the world, will be able to walk through or fly through 3D worlds or explore the virtual city of a proposed site to analyze contextual norms and scale. While you all view these sites, interactive, real-time design discussions can be conducted. If you wish to analyze similar cities, you will be able to jump from one VRML world to another, much like hot-linking through Internet home pages.

Rendered 3D architectural models created with a visualization application like 3D Studio MAX can be saved as VRML files. If your architecture firm, consultants, or clients have a World Wide Web home page on the Internet, this file can be uploaded to the respective home page, and members of the design team (or client) can remotely access, manipulate, and analyze the design by exploring a VR movie. The implication of this visualization technique is limitless—architects can collaborate as well as market their services globally using moving pictures, which more closely depict what the design is all about.

Several visualization applications such as 3D Studio Max, StudioPro Blitz, and Virtus Walkthrough Pro have already begun to integrate this technology into their software. This technology will have a major impact on the way architects share and visualize their designs, as well as market to potential clients in remote locations. There is great potential for VRML use within the AEC community. By way of illustration, most CADD and 3D models are constructed by putting components of the building on separate layers. For example, floor slab, exterior walls, roofing, and glazing would each be constructed on a separate layer. The software could link elements on different layers to other sites on the World Wide Web. Once a layer like roofing has been anchored or hyperlinked to a Web site such as AEC Information center (http://www.aecinfo.com), using a VRML browser like WebFX, you would be able to click on a layer of interest— roofing for instance—to access manufacturer information and suppliers to obtain current pricing and specifications.

Necessary Equipment

The beauty is that everything described here can be accomplished right from your Pentium desktop computer—you know, the one that's currently being used to crank out production drawings. Other than the software, you don't need additional hardware.

Step 1

From within Autodesk 3D Studio, the VRML plug-in is initialized, and a dialog similar to this one appears with all of the layers of the model listed under the Object Name column. Any of these layers can then be anchored to an Internet Web site. For this demonstration, we have linked the glass, walls, and slab layers to AEC InfoCenter Home Page, which has a library of building materials, contractors, cost analyses, and manufacturers.

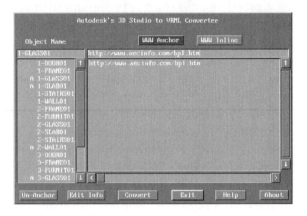

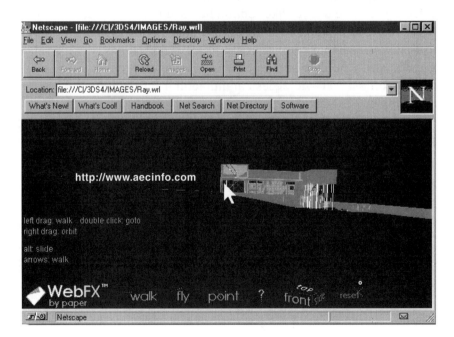

Step 2

Once the 3D Studio model is converted to a VRML format, it is then opened in Netscape. This process is virtually seamless because the WebFX VRML browser works as a plug-in within Netscape. As you can see when I moved the mouse over the glass of the building, the URL address, **http://www.aecinfo.com**, which will link you to the AEC InfoCenter Web site (home page), is displayed.

Step 3

During your presentation, clicking on various levels of the model will take you to more information on the Web like AEC's InfoCenter with its libraries of construction materials, building products, and suppliers.

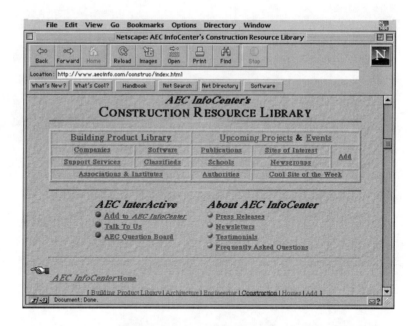

AN INDUSTRY OVERVIEW

Marketing is all about capturing attention and making an impact, and video is a high-impact medium. With the time restrictions placed on design presentations, many architects use it in their marketing efforts because it is visually appealing and optimal for communicating three-dimensional ideas within a defined period of time.

With desktop digital video, visual communicators like architects can create professional-quality video for marketing and training on a standard desktop computer. The benefit of digital video is that once it's created, it can be distributed in many ways. Your final video production can easily be "printed" to a VHS tape to show at your next client presentation. Or, the same composition can be kept in its digital format for distribution on CD-ROM or over the Internet. You can also take the finished video, drop it into your favorite authoring package to create an interactive CD-ROM for potential clients or post it on your Internet Web site so that cyberspace browsers can learn about your work. This range of output choices means that you can fully leverage your video assets.

The ability to accomplish this on the desktop is being fueled by:

- User-friendly software that allows users to create quickly and easily.
- The improving price/performance of the supporting hardware: video boards, storage devices, and desktop computers.

The leaps experienced in desktop video during the 1990s rival those seen in desktop publishing in the 1980s. What was once the domain of professionals working on dedicated systems that cost $50,000 to $100,000 can now be accomplished on standard desktop computers for under $10,000. Nontraditional creators of video, that is, architects and designers, can now use tools such as Avid Real Impact to produce their videos in-house just as they use desktop publishing packages such as PageMaker and Quark to publish articles or lay out 2D promotional materials.

Do you have to be a video expert to use this technology? Absolutely not. You just need to purchase a product whose designer assumed you are a computer-oriented person, not a video editing professional.

Tips before You Buy

To help you be most productive, your video editing software must:

- Run on standard desktop platforms such as IBM's standard Pentium processors.
- Integrate well with other packages an architect might use, such as Autodesk 3D Studio and AutoCAD, Bentley's MicroStation, Graphisoft's ArchiCAD, or Macromedia Director. You want to be able to seamlessly import completed models and animations from your favorite 3D package into video. Your video software must coexist well with your other desktop

applications—instability is not acceptable. It is extremely important that you find out from the manufacturer whether your existing applications would conflict with the desktop digital video system of your interest.

- Be easy to use. On-line help and tutorials are critical to getting the novice user up and running. Features such as drag/drop/play and 32 levels of undo/redo encourage creativity in addition to providing quick recovery from mistakes.
- Provide the flexibility for multiple output formats—create once, distribute in many ways.

It can be very cost-effective to create your own video. If you go to a professional video production outfit, it can cost up to $2,000 for one minute of finished video. On the other hand, today, you can add a product such as Avid's Real Impact and a Truevision Targa 2000 PCI board to your standard PC for approximately $6,500. Consequently, if you install Real Impact and a Targa 2000 PCI board in your Pentium and create more than four minutes of finished video, you've paid for your investment! Additionally, you get the control and flexibility that comes with creating your own content.

What Will the Future Bring?

Users will see expanded price/performance options. Additional video capture boards will provide alternatives for investment cost and quality. Distribution options will continue to increase with advances in high-density CD-ROMs and the Internet. We will also see improvements in compression technologies for Internet distribution. Today, the best formats for distribution over the Internet are .avi (Microsoft's Video for Windows video standard), QuickTime (Apple's Macintosh and Windows cross-platform format) and MPEG-1 encoded video. Internet users simply download the MPEG, AVI, or QT files from the Internet and play them back from their hard drive. Moreover, in the very near future we will be able to easily distribute digital video presentations, created in our offices, over the Internet and interact with clients remotely, in real time.

A SOFTWARE SOLUTION

You may be asking yourself how video technology can assist your firm in marketing your design services to existing and potential clients. If you want to gradually enter the realm of digital video, you can begin with user-friendly video capturing, editing, and special effects software like Adobe Premier and After Effects. Thanks to Sony Electronics, I am sure that someone in your office has a camcorder. And because your firm places great importance on producing accurate construction documents, you have a powerful 486, Pentium, Macintosh, or Power Macintosh computer in your office. The symbiosis of these dynamic technologies has given birth to Desktop Digital Video, which allows the recording, manipulation, storage, and playing back of video images as digital computer files. Now your firm can prepare marketing video presentations right from your desktop computer—the same powerful computer you purchased for CADD production in a concise and dynamic manner that was impossible to accomplish just a few years ago.

Before we look at how you can produce desktop digital video presentations using off-the-shelf software, let's explore some of the benefits of this marketing approach:

For beginners, we know that producing a digital marketing video can be less expensive than producing a four-color brochure.

 Video can deliver the greatest amount of information in the shortest amount of time. This becomes important when you consider that many public municipalities limit your presentation to a finite period of time.

 Video will give you the opportunity to evoke not only sight senses of your clients, but also sound and emotions. This can be accomplished through the use of a variety of visual images in conjunction with narrative and appropriate background music.

 Because of time constraints, many clients do not want to mull through lengthy brochures. They would rather spend the limited time they do have reviewing dynamic information in video form than static text on paper.

 The fact that almost every client or municipal review commission has access to a VCR and television makes video an attractive medium with which to market design services.

 Finally, digital video can encompass many other media. For example, 35mm slides, audio recording, computer-generated modeling, rendering, and animation walk-through, as well as graphic artwork can be easily integrated into one cohesive video presentation.

Now, let's say that you are short-listed for a project and you are given 15 minutes to present. You are excited. Your firm decides to jump into digital video, first trying the software solution. What do you do next?

Preparing and collecting footage:
(You are armed for battle with your camcorder and VCR.)

- You can videotape interviews of your principals discussing the firm's philosophy, past projects, and future goals.
- Videotape interviews of your design team discussing design concepts and solutions.
- Videotape the proposed site from several vantage points, and from the computer, superimpose this video footage with computer animations of your design solution on the proposed site.

Step 1 — Capturing Video

Since most Intel-based computers are not shipped with a video/audio capture board, (unlike most of Apple computers) you will need a board like Fast Electronic' FPS 60 in order to retrieve video and audio from a camera or VCR. Devices like the FPS 60 actually convert video analog to a digital signal for use on your computer.

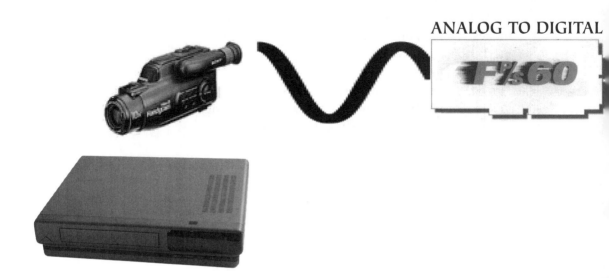

ANALOG TO DIGITAL

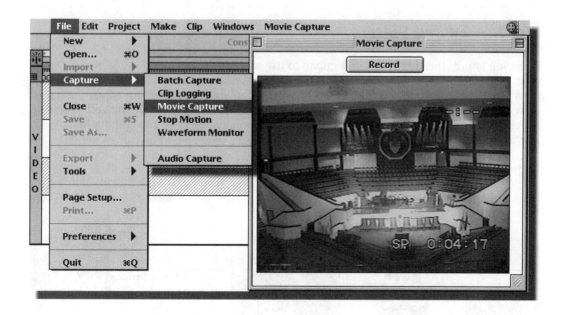

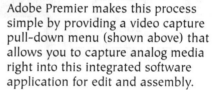

Adobe Premier makes this process
simple by providing a video capture
pull-down menu (shown above) that
allows you to capture analog media
right into this integrated software
application for edit and assembly.

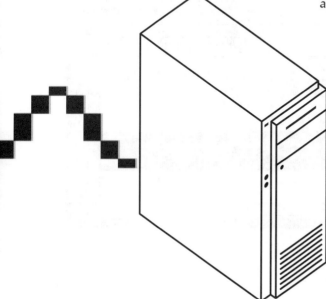

Step 2 — Editing Video

Once you import the video clips you intend to use into the Project Window, each clip can then be placed in the Video Track where they are viewed in a variety of segment increments, from 1 frame at a time to several minutes at a time, depending on how you adjust the time increments. From the Video Track, these clips can be edited with precision by cutting and splicing the appropriate segments for your presentation, enabling you to edit out bad or unwanted frames.

Import video clips into the Project Window.

Drag a transition into the T track between video clips.

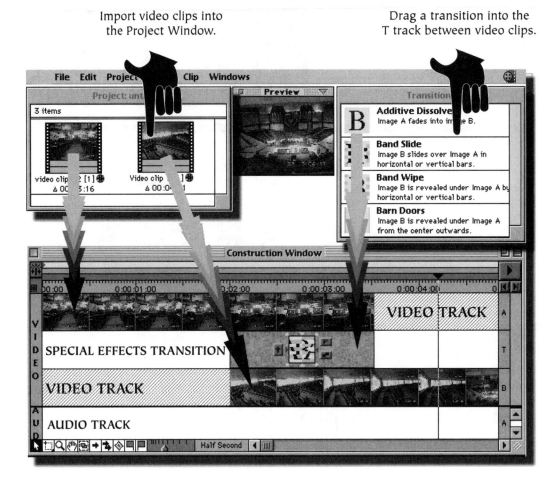

Step 3 — Adding Voice, Sound, Music

One of the great features of Adobe Premier is that it accepts a variety of media from different applications and platforms. On an Intel-based computer, you can again use Fast Electronic's FPS 60 card to capture voice, sound, and music, which is then converted to a digital signal, for enhancing the marketing video. However, Macromedia's SoundEdit provides us with the most flexible solution for voice, sound, and music on any Audio Visual (AV)-ready Macintosh computer. Files from SoundEdit can be imported into your digital video presentation being compiled in Adobe Premier, either on the Macintosh or Intel-based computers.

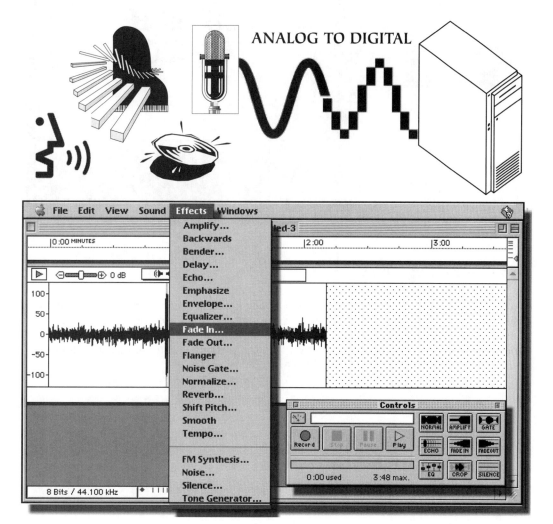

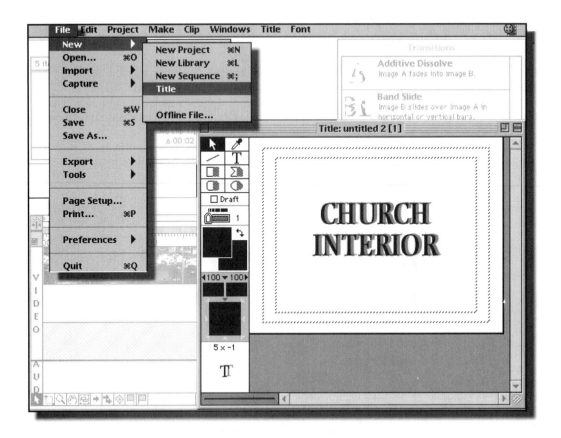

Step 4 — Adding Titles

By choosing New/Title from the File menu of Adobe Premier, you can create titles that will assist your clients to understand and follow your digital video presentation. From within Adobe's Title window, you can create both stationary and animated type, straight lines and various geometric shapes that can be used as titles. These titles can then be superimposed over clips in the Video Track to create titles and credits.

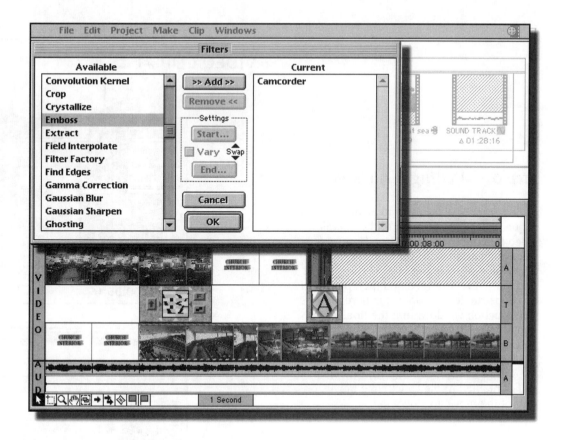

Step 5 — Adding Filters

Adobe Premier and Adobe After Effects include a variety of filters (similar to the ones you use in Photoshop) that can be applied to your video clips which, after all, are a series of still frames. These filters will let you distort, blur, emboss, sharpen, smooth, texture, and color images. Adobe Premier also includes audio filters such as the Echo filter, which produces an echo effect, and the Fill Left and Fill Right filters, which affect the spatial quality of the sound. In addition, Adobe Premier gives you the ability to create motion effects in movies and on still-image clips, which are similar to those achieved using an animation camera, such as zooming into an area of the video clip.

VIDEO CLIP #2
VIDEO CLIP #1

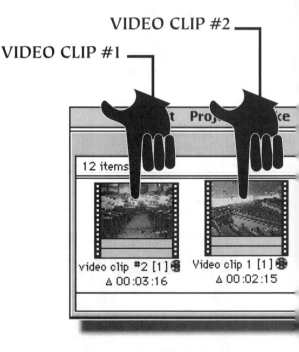

Step 6 — Putting It All Together

Adobe Premier allows you to arrange sequentially each element of the digital video into the Project window. Here, video, titles, animation walk-through, still renderings, voice-over, sound effects, transitions, and music are arranged and then placed in the Construction window. It is here, in the Construction window, that the final edited digital video is assembled. Once completed, you can play the final presentation on your IBM Pentium or Power Macintosh monitor or TV screen (NTSC), compile your movie as a self-contained Apple QuickTime movie, or output the movie to videotape.

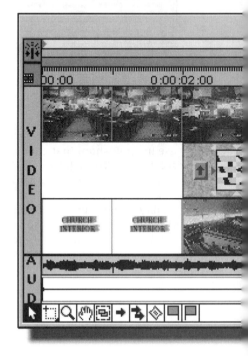

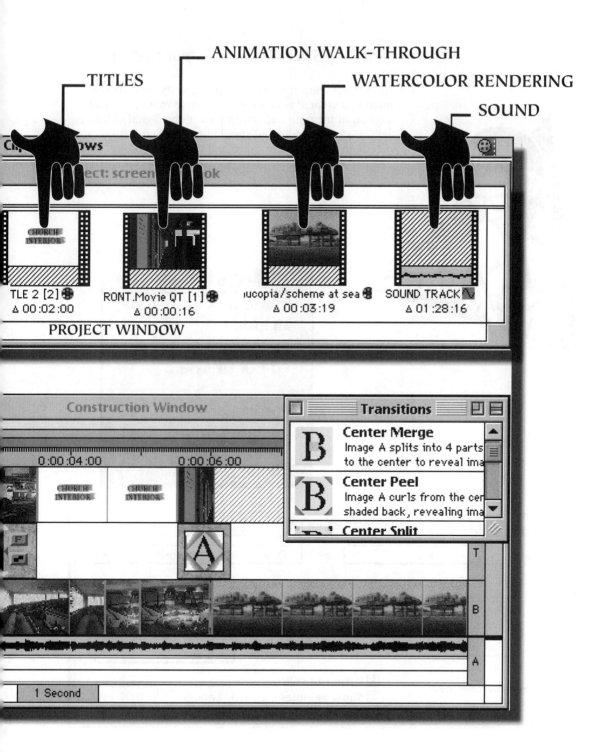

TITLES

ANIMATION WALK-THROUGH

WATERCOLOR RENDERING

SOUND

Clip Windows

ect: screen...ok

CHURCH INTERIOR

TLE 2 [2] ▲ 00:02:00

RONT.Movie QT [1] ▲ 00:00:16

ιucopia/scheme at sea ▲ 00:03:19

SOUND TRACK ▲ 01:28:16

PROJECT WINDOW

Construction Window

0:00:04:00   0:00:06:00

CHURCH INTERIOR   CHURCH INTERIOR

A

Transitions

Center Merge
Image A splits into 4 parts
to the center to reveal ima

Center Peel
Image A curls from the cer
shaded back, revealing ima

Center Split

T

B

A

1 Second

Step 7 — Select Project Output Option

The Project Output option lets you specify how the digital video you created is compiled. It is here that you specify the output file type and which part of the digital video in the Construction window should be compiled. Also, you specify the image output size and the audio quality.

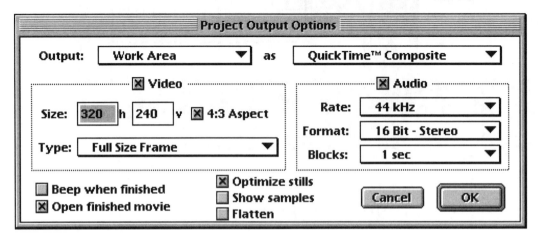

If you are using Adobe Premier on the PC, you will need an audio visual card such as Fast Electronic's FPS 60 (see right) in order to output your compiled Premier movie to videotape.

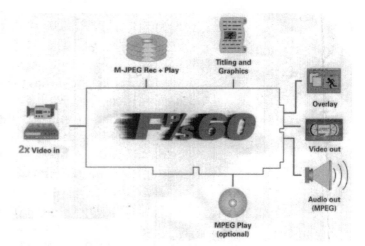

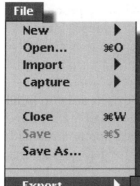

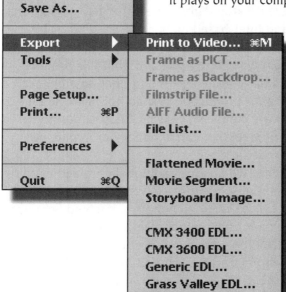

You can record a Premier movie sequence to videotape using the Print to Video command found under the File/ Export pull-down menu. All you need is a tape deck for recording the movie. Once the tape deck is connected to the audio visual card in your Power Macintosh or IBM Pentium, you can videotape the Adobe Premier movie in real time as it plays on your computer screen.

That's all there is to it! With your firm's desktop digital video in hand, you are ready to present to your client!

USING DIGITAL VIDEO IN WINDOWS

When we began researching desktop digital video for this book, it was important that the solution for architects and designers meet specific criteria. First of all, it was important that the manufacturer of this desktop digital solution be a company that had been in existence for a period of time during which it had made a significant contribution toward producing cutting-edge technology in this new industry. Second, it was our goal to present a product that was user-friendly enough so that anyone familiar with the operation of a PC could quickly learn how to produce desktop digital video marketing presentations. Third, we looked for a product as well as a company that was reliable and dependable. Fourth, it was important that the product integrate well with all of the other three-dimensional products that architects use. Next, in order to fulfill the needs of a growing diversified practice of architecture, we felt that it was important that the company presented here also have desktop digital video products on both the Macintosh and Intel-based platforms.

Finally, because we do not have an unlimited budget for marketing, I wanted to make sure that this product could be used on an existing Pentium that an architect might be using for production. We do not have the time to manage software conflicts; we want to use a desktop digital video product that can enhance our marketing efforts, not hinder it.

As architects, we are not traditionally trained as videographers. Consequently, we were very concerned about the fact that the product that's presented here not require significant training that would take us away from what we do best: practicing architecture.

After careful research, we found that Avid Technology, a pioneer in the use of digital video, was a company with a successful track record that could meet the needs of our industry. Over its seven-year history, Avid has helped thousands of video professionals, broadcasters, multimedia and communication professionals, and consumers to create finished video productions right on their desktops. With the introduction of Real Impact, Avid is bringing its Emmy- and Oscar-winning digital video-editing technology to Windows multimedia production.

Avid's Real Impact makes it easy for architects and designers to use digital video with PC-based multimedia productions. Real Impact brings many of the features of Avid's all-Mac line of products like Media Suite Pro to the Windows environment. This Windows-based product makes adding video to your marketing efforts an experience similar to working with Adobe PageMaker—you can be productive without the technical hastle of being a DOS, Windows, or video expert.

Add Video to Your Presentations

Your digital video-editing software can become the hub of your multimedia process. Then, dynamic multimedia production becomes a three-step process:

1. Gather video, 3D, animation, audio, graphic, and special effects content.
2. Edit them together in a digital video sequence. Add interactivity with your favorite authoring package.
3. Output this video sequence to tape or keep it in digital format for use in an interactive program for CD-ROM, network or Internet distribution.

The following sections detail these steps.

1. Gather Multimedia Content

Video

How about that stack of videotapes in your office? You probably have fantastic videos that were customized for the client of your last project. Digitize this footage onto the computer and use the content as the basis for your new video sequence. Also, like clip art, many professional, post-production facilities offer stock video footage with varied distribution rights. You can purchase video from these libraries or use your camcorder.

3D Graphics and Animation

Many multimedia producers use 3D graphics and animations from their favorite Windows applications to include in their digital video presentations. You can create animated logos, models of products, or simulated walk-throughs using such popular packages as Autodesk 3D Studio, Caligari trueSpace2, Macromedia Extreme 3D or MacroModel, Ray Dream Designer, or ElectricImage Animation.

Audio

You can capture 16-bit, 44.1 kHz CD-quality sound, and enhance your presentation with audio content such as voices and background noise, narration, and music and sound effects available from stock audio CD libraries.

Special Effects

Warps and morphs created with such packages as Avid Elastic Reality and Adobe After Effects can help you add creative wizardry to a multimedia production.

Edit—with Real Impact

Avid Real Impact, Avid Technology's award-winning 32-bit video-editing software for Windows NT multimedia production is a good "hub" for your multimedia creation process.

But isn't video difficult to edit? It doesn't have to be! *This software application is designed for communicators who have little or no experience making videos.*

Once you have your content, editing is as easy as drag, drop, and play. Simply drag video, graphics or audio to the time line; drop in clips; and play back your sequence instantly.

When your video story is complete, you're ready to "print" or use it in an interactive multimedia presentation.

A project window viewed using Avid's Real Impact Software.

Output for Your Audience

The benefit of digital video is that you can create once and distribute in many ways. Your final video production can easily be printed to a VHS tape.

With Real Impact, the same composition also can be kept in its digital format for video playback on the computer screen, whether that's an interactive CD-ROM, video clip inserted into a Microsoft PowerPoint presentation, video played back on an interactive kiosk, or PC-based workstation, or even just-in-time video information available on a corporate network or the Internet.

The Multimedia Production Process:

SHOOT AND CAPTURE VIDEO

ADD:

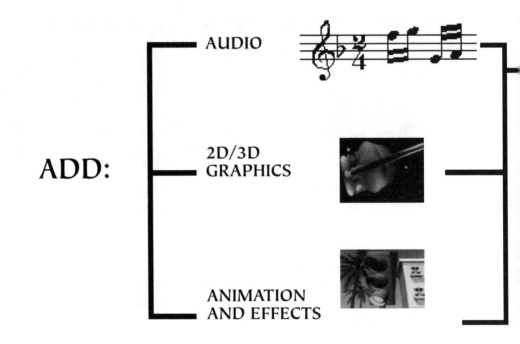

AUDIO

2D/3D GRAPHICS

ANIMATION AND EFFECTS

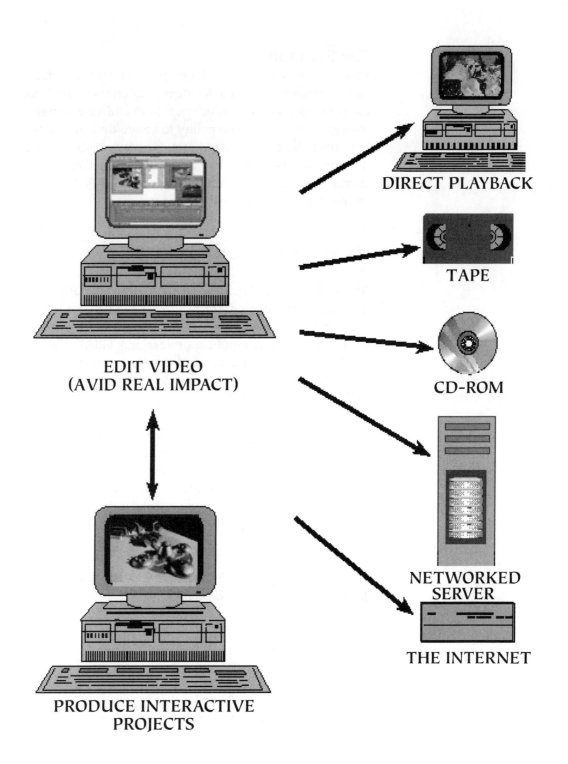

DIRECT PLAYBACK

TAPE

CD-ROM

EDIT VIDEO
(AVID REAL IMPACT)

NETWORKED
SERVER

THE INTERNET

PRODUCE INTERACTIVE
PROJECTS

The Solution

Video, audio, animations, 3D graphics and special effects can be combined into digital video sequences by multimedia creators seeking to educate, inform and/or entertain with greater impact. The ability to create dynamic content, once the domain of experts, is now available on the desktop for widespread use for a range of applications. Working on a presentation program on your PC? Add edited video clips for greater impact.

USING TRADITIONAL VIDEO

Although desktop digital video production is relatively new, larger architectural firms have been using traditional video in their marketing efforts for some time. So, in order to educate ourselves on how professional video production companies have addressed the marketing needs of these large design firms, we sat down for an interview with the president of MultiVision, a video production company located in Coral Gables, Florida. Bob Berkowitz has been producing marketing video presentations for architectural firms and Fortune 500 companies for the past 25 years. He agreed to talk with us about the ways in which some of his architectural clients make use of video presentation techniques to win clients. It proved to be an education in the art of story-telling and presentation. Read on and learn more.

Real-Life Tips on Marketing with Video
Interview With Bob Berkowitz

CC: Curtis B. Charles
BB: Bob Berkowitz

BB: Early in our company's evolution, architects realized that we were very good at selling image, selling the ideas and turning them into reality in front of a prospective client. This is before the age of computerization and three-dimensional modeling and computerized presentations. In those days, we would start with everything from blueprints and simple renderings, and we would turn them into slide shows and multiprojector visions of a finished project. Architects always needed some form of drama to bring projects and concepts to life, and it's something we've always been pretty good at.

I've always been pretty good at telling a story, so the architecture firms that we've dealt with are those that realize our talents were in the story-telling side, transferring what they do into a story that could excite an audience. So architecture firms would come to us and say, here's our unique selling proposition as we see it. This is the competition, and here is the committee and the players; what do we say to them? And we would look at those elements and play devil's advocate, and we would tell them where we thought they were weak. Then they would come up with a way to combat that weakness and, finally, we would create an entire presentation.

The traditional pitch has a set time limit, set theatrical parameters, and it has some very well-designed equalizing factors. We were able to capitalize on a certain client's persona, personality, and ego to create some pretty impressive showbiz-type presentations that really told a story.

CC: One thing I am interested in is that architects usually get short-listed; that is, they're told please feel free to take a specific project and present yourself. Then, once they're selected, they need to make this presentation to a design review board or something; how does that scenario work? The other issue I want to touch on is using video for marketing as compared with foamcore boards.

BB: As to being short-listed, that's something that is very hard to pinpoint but there are a whole bunch of considerations: political, knowing the turf, knowing the field, knowing what you must say about yourself and your work, knowing the team you must put together to get a given job, and knowing the political and socioeconomic relationships between the people on the selection committee.

CC: And how does video help?

BB: The creativity pitch comes after the shortlist; the shortlist is really honing your skills as an architect until you know you can make it X percent of time with a given set of parameters. Then, break down your presentation in strategic increments of five minutes, where no single piece is over five minutes; no single speaker should have more than five minutes. You can address a topic for more than five minutes but you should change the presenter at least to break the monotony. A single presenter tends to bore an audience.

In terms of producing the material, we have always found that leading off with story-telling helps present who the team is and what its credentials are. I find that a canned piece works better than someone standing up and saying we did this project and that project; it also gives a third-party endorsement, even though it's some paid announcer. There is something impressive about hearing an announcer talking about your firm and your capabilities. It comes off very well in terms of introducing the team and the team's strengths.

CC: How have you seen the type of video service you provide enhance or complement architecture marketing? Has it made a difference in getting jobs? What is the added service you bring?

BB: The presentation will not get you the job if you are not close, but it can put you over the edge if you are. Many times in governmental bids it depends on the way the rankings go; it is a closed ranking system. You've got seven or eight strangers or relative strangers ranking what you are saying. You should be fully cognizant of the point structure and how it works and where you are strong and where you are weak. The question is how to make sure you can get you those extra .75 points, that extra point and a half. Where I think we make a difference is in that extra 5-10 point range.

CC: You think video gives a firm the opportunity to raise the point spread?

BB: I think it does. I think it gives an increased sense of your professionalism. It can accentuate the positive and really set a tone for the rest of the pitch, and that's what I think the opening piece can do. One of the most important things it can do is eliminate the not great segments of your architects and engineers. I can't tell you how many times I've seen architects and engineers go into techno-talk in front of a nontechnical audience. To me that's one of the greatest mistakes they can make. And with a canned presentation you edit out the unnecessary portions.

CC: What do you think is probably the most challenging or most memorable architectural presentation you have done?

BB: We've done several pitches for firms who have designed airports. We've pitched some rather large international airport projects to large government agencies. We've done things with laser discs that were interactive where the audience could actually drive some of the responses to the question. Those are kinds of the things I find memorable. We've also done quite a bit locally for a firm who's done a lot of educational work. I find that interesting because colleges and universities pose such an interesting architectural challenge. The pitch is very political and it brings up some interesting design and layout-type projects where you can do some very nice multimedia-type things. We've done pitches for big theatrical shows for 20, 30, 40 people; and other times it's six people. You have to set the scale by which you work. If you tell me you have three people and it's a government project and they are engineers, I don't want to come in with too much whiz-bang because they get turned off by it; they think you are not substantive. I've seen other situations where the architect has misread it the other way, and one of the competitors came in with whiz-bang, wowed the committee, and went all the way. It's a tough business; there's no sure-fire thing here, but I'll tell you, by and large you have to be careful in smaller venues not to overdo it.

CC: This brings me to probably my last two questions. Why should an architecture firm trying to market its services use video versus traditional presentations? What's the advantage—in a nutshell?

BB: I think the advantage is image, image, image! When it comes to the substantive side of things, there is a lot to be said for showing three-dimensional graphics and modeling and all the things you are doing. I think it is really good in its place.

CC: Are your video and communication services only for large firms, or can smaller firms take advantage as well?

BB: Traditionally, large firms have been able to spend the money; not that we are expensive, but the whole question is whether they can do it or do it right. Is it for larger firms? It's for larger firms on a regular basis, smaller firms who see the value of getting work. It costs money to make money. It's an investment like a brochure, like your logo, like the facade of your building, like anything else—it sets the tone of who you are. For us, it has become a marketing priority for a lot of architecture firms. We would like to see more of it. Many architecture firms prefer to keep graphics and the presentation side of the business in-house where they think they have control.

Online
Marketing

T he Internet! The Internet! The Internet! It's everywhere. You cannot escape it. Your staff, colleagues, clients, spouses, and even children ask "What's your e-mail address?" "What's your URL? Visited any new sites lately? Did you FTP the drawings to the structural engineer's office? Did you use Gopher to retrieve the specifications of that Lo Emissivity glass? How many potential clients visited your home page this week?"

It's enough to drive you crazy! A busy architect like you has more pressing issues to deal with—programming, schedules, design, construction documents, change orders, and demanding clients. The information superhighway; love it or hate it, it's here to stay. You may be confused by all the hype. You have so many questions. What is the Inter-

net? What is it used for? How can it help my business? How can I get connected?

Well, unless you have worked for the defense department or have conducted research at a university, the Internet and all its potential is probably new to you. Those of us who have attended research-oriented architecture institutions like MIT, have long understood the impact the Internet can have on our profession, especially in marketing and remote design collaborations. This portion of the book will weave through all the hype and jargon of the Internet and give you an overview of how your design firm can maximize its marketing efforts by taking advantage of the multitude of resources available on the Internet.

What Is It?

The Internet, also known as the Net, is extremely difficult to define, because it means different things to different people. To some, the Internet is a service from which information can be retrieved through interconnected networks of computers. To others, the Internet is a community in which there is a cooperative effort by many people and organizations who work together to use and enhance the networks. However, it is important to note that the Internet is not a single entity, managed by any one agency or corporation.

History

Back in the late '60s the United States Department of Defense launched a program to investigate techniques and technologies for the interlinking of computer networks of various kinds. The objective of this program was to allow networked computers to transfer information rapidly and securely in times of war and national emergencies. Soon after, the network was extended to include universities and defense contractors.

Description

The National Center for Super Computing Applications (NCSCA) describes the Internet as being a complex global network consisting of thousands of independent computer networks administered by private businesses, government agencies, and educational and research institutions. The Internet can be thought of as a set of standards that enable communications between public and private networks running over any medium—phone lines, traditional network lines, fiber optic and even cable television wires, and wireless systems. It is also platform-independent, running across PCs, Macintoshes, workstations, and mainframes. A computer and a modem is all the hardware you need to be able to connect your firm to the Internet.

Definition

Many authors have defined the Net as a network formed by the cooperative interconnection of computing networks that consist of a mind-boggling number of participants, connected machines, software programs, and massive quantities of information, spread around the world. Although this is the correct scientific and technological definition to describe the Internet, the concept is difficult to grasp. I prefer Smith and Gibbs' analogy: "Imagine yourself as a navigator out on the ocean. You are surrounded by islands, and you can see hundreds of lighthouses marking ports and towns. What's worth sailing over to? What's going to be interesting and useful?" That is the Net. An ocean of information located at a multitude of different sites, available to anyone who wants to make the voyage.

WWW

World Wide Web Browsers

The World Wide Web is part of the Internet. In order to navigate the Web, you need what is called a browser. In short, browsers are based on a graphical user interface (GUI) similar to that of the Macintosh Operating System and Windows 95. One of the first browsers on the Internet was developed by staff and students at the University of Illinois' National Center for Super Computing Applications (NCSA) in 1993. This product was called NCSA Mosaic. The immediate success of this free navigation software developed into a commercial application called Netscape Navigator, and it has gone on to become the leader of the pack of stand-alone browsers, claiming about 75 percent of the browser market. This Web product is steadily becoming the standard for navigating as well as doing business on the Internet.

"Surfing the Net"

Actually, like many, when I first began navigating the Internet, I too felt as if I was drifting in the ocean. I was lost in "cyberspace" and did not know how I was going to find my way. If you have lots of time on your hands, you can spend hours surfing the Net. The key to the Internet is knowing where to look for the information you want to retrieve, and more important, if you choose to use the Internet as a marketing device, how potential clients will find you. Unfortunately, this is presently one of the problems of the Internet. It lacks structure, perhaps because it is not owned by any one organization or corporation. This means that there is no complete directory of available services, no instruction manual, no 1-800 technical support service to assist often frustrated new users. Nevertheless, it continues to appeal to and attract new users in record numbers. It is estimated that there are currently 35 million people connected to the Internet.

Regardless of your views on the viability of the Net as a good marketing forum for design services, these numbers must tempt even the most skeptical. Furthermore, during testimony to the U.S. House of Representatives, Vinton Cerf, a pioneer of the Internet, projected that by the year 1998 the Internet's population will exceed 100 million. Internet-based marketing is in its infancy, and design firms that decide to invest in it should recognize that it's an investment for the future.

What Is It Used For?

Even with this astounding growth, electronic mail or e-mail continues to be the most commonly used aspect of the Internet. With electronic mail, you can send a message to a remote computer without requiring that your client, colleague, or consultant be at the destination computer system at the time the remote system actually receives the e-mail. In other words, e-mail is more like "talking" to an answering machine or a voice mail system than a telephone conversation.

Traditional Mail vs. Electronic Mail

E-mail is similar to the mail or package delivered by Federal Express, UPS, or the postal service. Whichever of these providers you may use to send mail there are several rituals you perform that are very similar to what happens when sending electronic mail.

1. *Compose mail.*

2. *Address envelope.*

3. *Mail.*

4. *Deliver by carrier.*

5. *Return to sender if undeliverable.*

Each of these steps can be used to describe both electronic mail and regular mail. The difference is in the content—electronic files versus printed material and the mail carrier—USPS, Federal Express, UPS versus CompuServe, MCI Mail, America Online. E-mail is delivered almost immediately while traditional mail, even express service, takes overnight. On the down side, there are certain things you just can't e-mail; for example, if you sold products or goods, instead of services.

Research

Beyond e-mail, your business can access information such as current global demographics, and financial, climatic, and environmental conditions from government agencies, libraries, and educational institutions. All this data and more can be obtained in a variety of ways. The simplest method is to use one of the many search engines available on the Web such as Yahoo or InfoSeek. For example: Your firm is designing a custom wood construction house, and you need information on windows and doors, such as manufacturer, specs, and costs

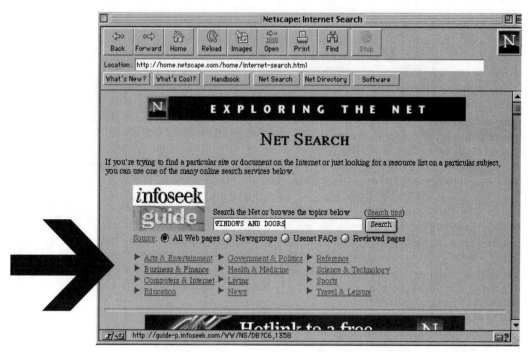

An InfoSeek search screen. You can search different areas of the Net. Each of the topics (Business & Finance, Living, News) is a link to those areas.

for the client who is in your office now!

You sign on to the Net, go to InfoSeek and type windows and doors, and click on Search. That will bring up several options. You choose one of them, Pella Windows and Doors.

Instead of scheduling another meeting with your client, you are able to take a look at the possibilities, pricing, and availability, on the spot. The client is able to make an informed decision immediately. You've saved time, impressed your client and, most important, you are able to complete the project on time. Your efficiency has impressed your client and made you a "lock" for any repeat business and referrals.

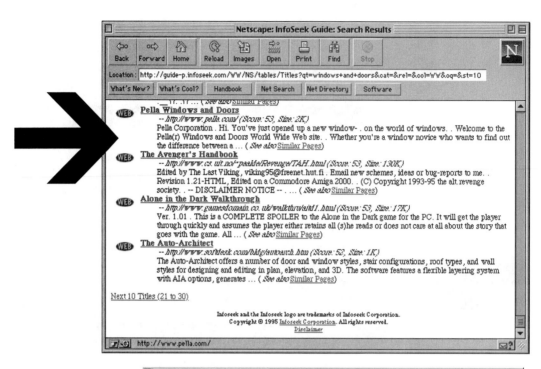

Information about window and door products can be found on the WWW.

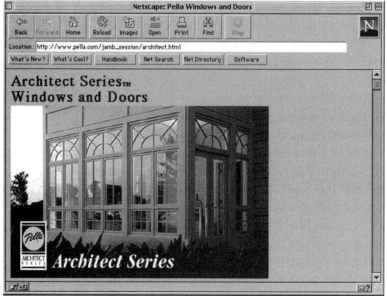

THE WORLD WIDE WEB

Earlier we said that the key to the Internet is knowing where to look for the information you want to retrieve. Well, the most productive way to retrieve information from the Internet is to browse the World Wide Web (WWW or the Web). The Web provides the easiest, most intuitive user interface for navigating the Internet. The World Wide Web was originally developed at CERN, the high-energy physics research center in Switzerland, as a hypertext system to facilitate information sharing worldwide.

The phenomenal growth of the Internet is largely credited to the Web, and can be traced back to its public availability in 1991. Because of this success, many users mistakenly refer to the Web as the Internet, and use the words interchangeably. The fact is, the World Wide Web is simply a new way of looking at the Internet, analogous to the manner in which the Windows graphical user interface (GUI) simplified DOS-based computing.

The Web uses a language called hypertext markup language, or HTML for short, to display text and graphics through your browser. The WWW protocol is based on a concept of linking that allows you to connect to various servers widely dispersed throughout the world, retrieve information you want, and return to your PC, by clicking the mouse, pressing an arrow key, or by typing a URL address in order to access the *home page* of a desired site. URLs are the resource locators used by 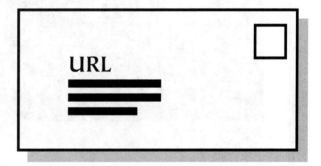 the World Wide Web as explicit addresses for information. These explicit strings are used by Web traversing programs to connect the user directly to a particular document or company's home page located on one of the many computers connected to the Internet.

I know many of you still need to be convinced. On the following pages, we will show you some examples of sites where you can find useful business information and some architecture firms already on the Net. Maybe you'll recognize your competition! More important, it will give you a better idea of what's available and how you could use the Net to benefit your firm.

WEB SITES OF INTEREST

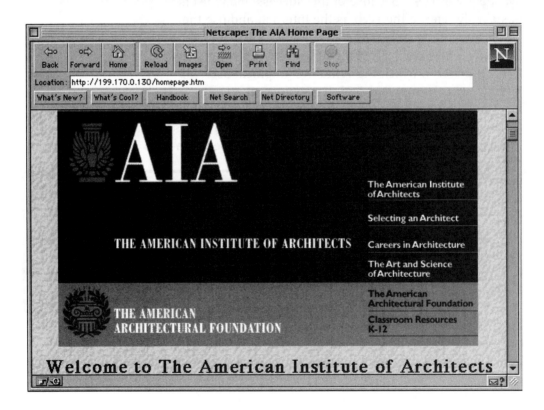

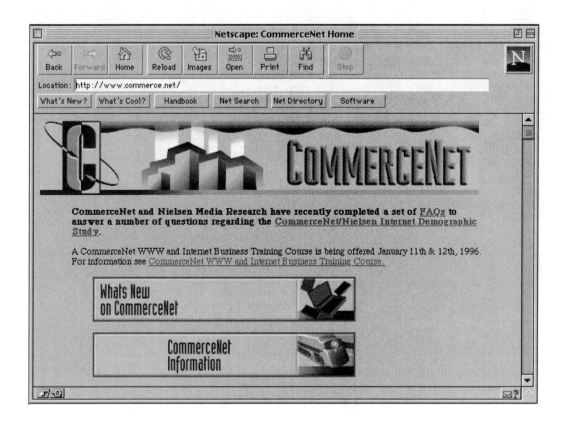

Above: This page provides information about doing business on the Net. It has links to a variety of business-related sites of interest.

Left: An old familiar face is on the Net. The AIA site offers information to the public at large about architecture and offers links to the home pages of other AIA-registered architects on the Net.

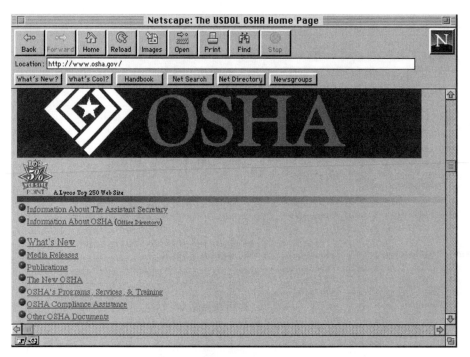

Through OSHA online, you can access info about programs, publications, and services.

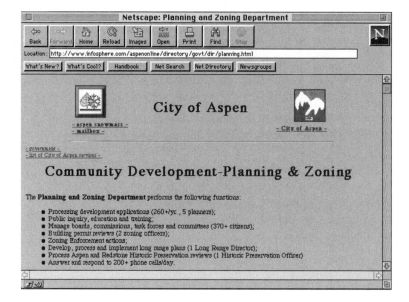

Some cities offer information about their planning and zoning departments. Soon, online submission and reviews will appear.

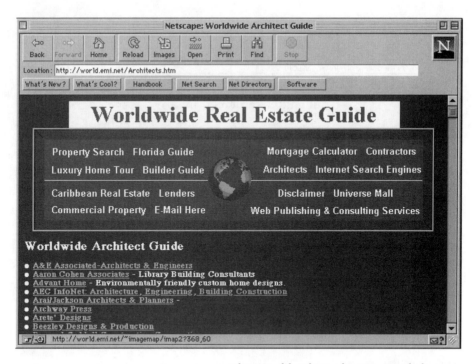

This Worldwide Real Estate Guide has an extensive listing of architects on the Web.

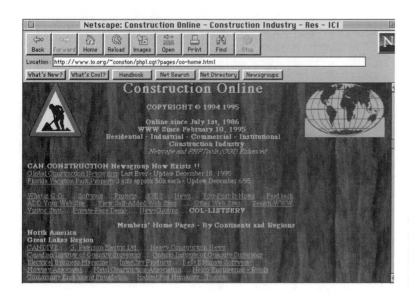

Construction Online serves as a meeting place and a source of information for people in the field.

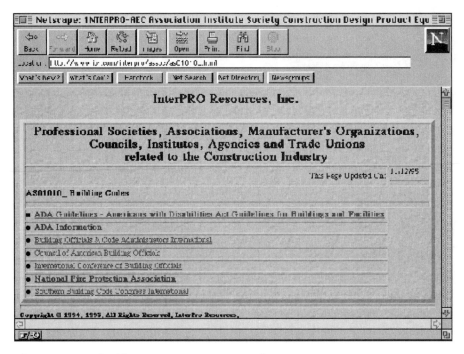

This site is a valuable resource containing information
pertaining to the Americans with Disabilities Act.
These guidelines impact your design of public facilities.

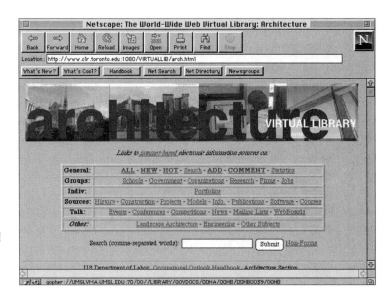

This virtual architectural
library gives you a wide
range of topics from
which to choose.

GETTING CONNECTED

Now that you have seen and understand the benefits of the Internet in general and the Web in particular, the next question is how to get connected. There are several ways that your firm can connect and gain access to the Internet. The two simplest ways are through a gateway on one of the popular online services, CompuServe or America Online, or through a local Internet service provider. Going through an online service allows only limited access and is a more expensive way to go, but you do not have to install software or follow sometimes complex directions before gaining access to the Net. An Internet service provider sells you access through his or her server at a far more competitive rate but you must have, at minimum, a working knowledge of your DOS, Windows, or Macintosh operating system. You should make the choice based on your personal level of experience.

Access through Commercial Online Services

Before the Internet's mass popularity there were online commercial services and bulletin boards. Some of the pioneering online services were CompuServe, America Online, Prodigy, Delphi, and GEnie. Over the past few years these online services have begun to provide Internet access to their members by acting as a gateway. Through this type of Internet access, your computer is not directly connected to the Internet; it is one of many terminals connected to another computer, which is itself attached to the Internet. In other words, you will have an indirect connection to the Internet. This type of access can be limiting when compared to the type of access that you can obtain from an Internet service provider. It is important to note, however, that the competition from other service providers is forcing rapid improvement in the quality of their Internet gateway services.

Internet Service Providers

As the Internet gains popularity, service providers are popping-up like mushrooms. As with every major business decision you make, it is advisable to do your research before making your selection. You choose based not only on the price but also time allowed, Web site creation and maintenance, and so on. You'll find many different combinations so, select the options that best suit your business. Service providers will allow your firm the most direct connection to the Internet. All you need is a computer and modem.

Establishing an Internet Account

Once you have decided upon an Internet provider, the first step is to fill an Internet Account-New User Information form. Here you will give the provider pertinent information including your company's name, credit card number, your computer operating system (Windows, Windows 95, NT, OS/2, Mac OS, or UNIX), user name and password desired (see the sample form on page 142). After you have been approved, you will be given an Internet account, which will allow your firm access to the Internet 24 hours a day, 7 days a week, 365 days a year. For this type of access, you may be charged a setup fee and then a flat monthly fee.

For this book we simulated the process of getting access to the Net by using Netpoint Communications, Inc., as a case study:

- You are given the appropriate software to set up your account.
- You do not need a specialist to install the software and set up your account.
- This Internet service provider does not charge any setup fee for Internet access.
- A monthly fee of $25.00 is charged for this access.
- You are allowed 100 hours of access time. There will be a charge for any time beyond these 100 hours.

Netpoint Communications, Inc.
Internet Accounts - New User Information

Date: ___/___/___

Name: _____

Address: _____

_____

City: _____ State: _____ Zip: _____

Phone: (___) ____-_____ Fax: (___) ____-_____

Is this a corporate account? ☐ Yes ☐ No

   If yes, Company Name: _____

Credit Card Information: ☐ Visa ☐ MasterCard ☐ Discover

   Number: _____ Expiration: _____

Have you accesed the Internet before? ☐ Yes ☐ No

   If yes, type of account: ☐ Shell ☐ SLIP/PPP ☐ Not Sure/Don't Know

                    ☐ Online Service (AOL, Compuserve, Prodigy)

Operating System: ☐ Windows ☐ Windows 95 ☐ NT ☐ OS/2 ☐ Mac OS

                  ☐ UNIX type: _____ ☐ Other: _____

Username: The username will indicate the name of your account. It consists of up to eight (8) lowercase letters and numbers. Your Internet address will be username@netpoint.net (e.g., jdoe@netpoint.net). Please provide three (3) choices in order of preference.

   Choice 1 (use if available): _____

   Choice 2 (use if 1 is not available): _____

   Choice 3 (use if 2 is not available): _____

Password: The password is used to authenticate your username. It should be at least six letters and numbers. It will be assigned to you over the phone. Do not share your password with others.

How did you hear about Netpoint? _____

_____

Please mail or fax the completed form to: Netpoint Communications, Inc.
                                       11077 Biscayne Blvd., Suite 304
                                       Miami, FL 33161

                                       Phone: (305) 891-1955   Fax: (305) 891-2110

This is an example of a typical form that an Internet service provider will require you to fill out before acquiring Internet access.

- You are given a PPP (Point-to-Point Protocol) dial-in account.
- Since this service is not proprietary, you can use any of the more popular Internet tools and browsers such as Netscape.
- Unlike some commercial online services, you get full access to all Internet tools and applications.
- You have the ability to conduct and control your virtual marketing efforts, by creating and maintaining a World Wide Web commercial site right from the comfort of your office, on your computer's hard drive.

THE FUTURE OF ONLINE ARCHITECTURE

The following interview is with Erick Valle, Professor of Architecture at the University of Miami, Coral Gables, Florida.

CC: Curtis Charles
EV: Erick Valle

CC: Erick, in this part of the book we have introduced the Internet as a medium architects can use to indirectly as well as directly market their design services. As an architect, a professor of this technology, and a planner of Cyber Cities, what is your interpretation of this technology called the Internet? What is your vision?

EV: First let me define what the Internet is. To me the Internet is a collaborative working environment, and that point is essential. It builds on this whole ideology, this belief, that if it's a working environment, we are going to be able to collaborate and have certain levels of interaction over the Internet. This is crucial to this whole concept of telepresence. Telepresence is in essence not having to be present at any one location, yet be able to interact in a group environment. That is where I see a lot of this technology going.

Furthermore, what we see when we visit a lot of sites on the Internet is that they are very static, two-dimensional sites. The technology is out there today to bring much more interaction and emotion to it. We can see sights now that have animated logos, and there is a very exciting aspect to it. One such is Apple where they have you visit Apple City where you see a series of buildings, and you can, just by putting your cursor over a building, cause things to move in different directions. On top of that you can also integrate sound, which obviously enhances the environment. The Internet itself has many other aspects that are very exciting. Being able to enter and have a presence on the Internet will literally make it a virtual environment in which you can walk and explore.

CC: Do you see that as a potential marketing tool?

Erick: Absolutely! Say I am the potential client who's interested in firms that do shopping centers. I go to the Internet, and I perform a search for architects who design shopping centers, and up pops those firms. Then I have the capability to actually log on to that firm and enter its virtual office. That in itself is an exciting opportunity. Just by looking at the building I am entering enables me to understand the caliber and character of the firm.

Then I can navigate and go into the drawing files of the firm and open up the file of a particular type of shopping mall in one area of the country. It shows me photographs of it, and I can click on a particular photograph of that shopping center and see video clips. Or, maybe using QuickTime VR, I choose to walk around the real place. That's an incredible way of showing a client clearly what the capabilities of that firm are.

CC: Isn't there a security risk for architects who make this kind of information public?

EV: Part of what firms sell is themselves, not only their ability to produce a great design, but within a certain budget. It is all relevant information that architects will want to expose.

CC: Do you think that being on the Internet will increase client base, or will this just be a tool to communicate remotely and access information?

EV: By the year 2000, if you don't have an Internet presence, you will not be in business. I venture to say that your Internet presence will be of greater importance than your physical address. If you do not have an Internet presence, you will be cut off from global marketing. For instance, I might need an engineer who does acoustics a certain way, and I can go and find him or her and interact over the Internet and not have to incur travel and time expenses.

CC: The concept of time and the ability to send files to different time zones is an interesting prospect. Could you elaborate on that?

EV: One model that is evolving is that of the firm that has offices in different parts of the world through a presence on the Internet. For example, I am in one time zone and my employees come in, work on a project, transfer the files to the Internet; the office in another time zone 12 hours later is coming in to work; they pick up this project and continue working on it. It happens again in a third time zone. By the time my time zone starts again the next physical day, work has already gone through literally two more days of work. So in a one-day period, you might literally be able to reproduce three days of work. This has incredible implications on production and the capability to explore alternatives in design. This concept of firms opening offices in three time zones can also cut costs.

Multimedia

Chapter 5

OVERVIEW

Multimedia is a combination of text, graphics, animation, audio, and video in an interactive environment. Used properly, multimedia can bring tremendous benefits to your marketing efforts. It will enable you to demonstrate your products and explain the services your company offers. It can represent you better than any individual, static media, including brochures or letters, ever will. A multimedia presentation allows you to take advantage of many different types of media and interactivity to educate customers about your products and services, ultimately leading to a sale or commission.

A well-designed multimedia presentation will get your clients' attention and improve their retention of the ideas contained therein, at a rate that is two to three times that of static presentations!

In the design field, we make extensive use of presentations to illustrate our ideas and demonstrate past projects to our clients. Previously, those presentations consisted of slides, boards, or even video. In this chapter, we introduce you to the world of multimedia and show you how it will change, for the better, the way you market to your clients now and in the future.

Designing a multimedia presentation is a lot like designing a building. It consists of several stages analogous to the phases involved in designing a building.

Planning and Programming

The planning stage of a multimedia project can be compared to the programming and conceptual design phases of a design project. You define the project—the purpose, the target audience, and the desired response. Then, armed with this information, you formulate a design concept. An important early consideration is the delivery platform. If you are going to deliver the project on a 3.5 inch diskette, the restrictions are different from a project that is to be delivered on a laptop computer or a CD-ROM.

File Formats

Different applications have different requirements with regard to file formats. It is important to take note of the file formats that your multimedia application will support or accept. Your CAD application may give you one type of file, say TIFF, but your multimedia software application will only accept PICT files. What do you do?

Depending on your software library, you have a couple of options. If you own an image-editing application like Photoshop or Photostyler, you could open the TIFF file in the image-editing application then save it as a PICT file. This is because both these packages offer the ability to

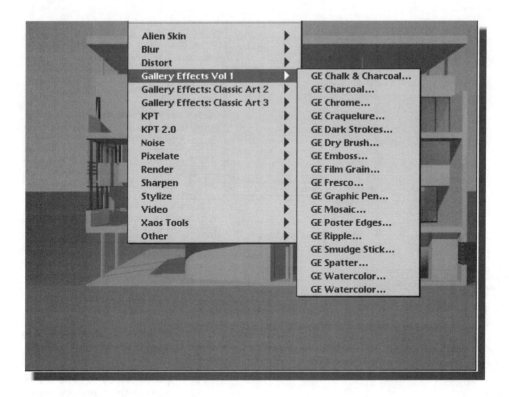

save a file as a number of different file types. If you own one of these image-editing applications, you can alter the image while you are in the application doing things like applying a watercolor filter or a blur.

The other option is a file conversion utility like DeBabelizer to convert the file from one type to another. DeBabelizer is a very useful conversion utility that will convert not only your graphic files, but also audio and animation files. It converts to and from a number of common and some not so common file formats. This utility will prove invaluable to us in the preparation of our digital files. If you haven't already run into problems with file conversion, count yourself lucky. When you deal with moving digital files from one application to another, you will frequently have file format problems, and you will come to appreciate DeBabelizer.

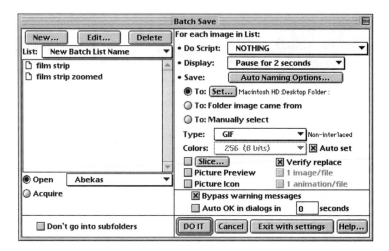

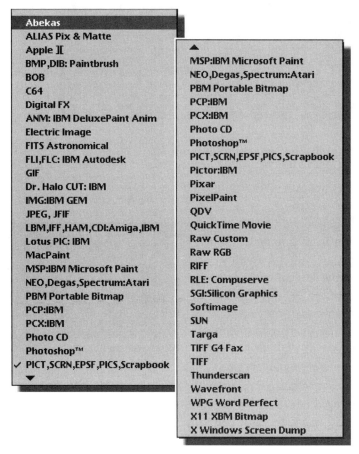

This is a list of the file formats DeBabelizer can handle. You may recognize some of them like the .fli or .flc animation files produced by 3D Studio, as well as the more common .pict and .epsf (encapsulated post script file). JPEG and GIF are the two formats in which graphics can be displayed on the Net. In creating Web pages, later on, you will need to convert your graphics from formats like .pcx, .pict, or .bmp to those two formats. For those of you who use workstations like Silicon Graphics or SUN, DeBabelizer also recognizes those file formats.

Lorem Ipsum

- **Delor sit amet consectetuer adipiscing elit sed diam**
  - Nonummy nibh euismod
    - Tincidunt ut; Laoreet dolore
    - Laoreet dolore; Tincidunt ut
    - Tincidunt ut; Magna aliquam
  - Magna aliquam
- **Exerci tation ullamcorper suscipit lobortis nisl ut aliquip ex ea com**
- **Delor sit amet consectetuer adipiscing elit sed**

Imagine having to read a slide like this in under one minute. (Granted, it would help if it were in English!). Remember, a picture really is worth 1,000 words.

Text

Text used in your multimedia presentation originates from many of the same sources you use in desktop publishing. (See Chapter 1, "Desktop Publishing," for an in-depth discussion of these sources.) It is important to remember not to make your multimedia presentation too text heavy for a couple of reasons.

- The ideas you want to convey will be presented not only in text but in graphics, video, and animation. Consequently, there is not a need for as much text as you would find in something like a brochure.
- The presentation is dynamic—in motion—so there is not a lot of time for reading large bodies of text. In your presentation, text will be used for captions, titles, headlines, and short explanations that support rather than detract from the rest of your presentation.

Graphics

The graphics you use in your multimedia presentation may originate from a variety of sources. Your CAD files, renderings, photographs, and clip art can all be included in your multimedia presentation. Almost all your CAD files will allow you to save your sheet to disk as a PICT file or some other format. The same is true for renderings. (Remember, format is not a big issue because we can always convert it later.)

If, for some reason, you cannot save out, you have the option of using a screen capture utility to take a screen shot, which is literally a picture of the screen. Many of the computer screen shots you see in this book were taken using this technique. Flash-It on the Mac and Grabber on the PC are just two examples of available applications.

To use photographs, you have a few options. First, you can scan your pictures using a flatbed or handheld scanner. You can scan color or black and white images of your project and site.

Second, you can use a digital camera. The camera looks like a regular camera but, instead of film, it saves your image as a digital file.

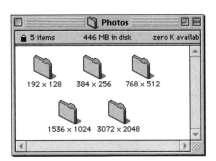

You then download the images to your computer. Apple and Kodak both make their own version of a digital camera.

Your third option involves using a regular camera then having your film developed on Photo CD, an option available at most film developing outlets. A photo CD has your photograph digitized to CD at five different resolutions for use in your presentation. This is a reasonable substitute for a scanner if the majority of your graphics will consist of photographs.

If you need other pre-digitized photographs, Image Club offers a series of CD-ROMs full of digitized graphics for every occasion. A related option is clip art. It comes already digitized on diskette or CD. Again, the topics are numerous, and you will be able to find something to match the theme of your presentation. (Much of the clip art used in this book can be purchased from Image Club.)

Audio

Audio accompanying a presentation can bring that presentation to life.

A multimedia title, like movies and television, just isn't the same without music and sound effects. Can you imagine the *Sound of Music* without the sound of music; *The Pink Panther* without Henry Mancini's sound track? It just wouldn't be the same! Improvements in theater and television sound systems such as surround sound reflect the importance of sound in creating the ambiance for a presentation. In a multimedia title, sound is used in much the same way. It enhances interactivity by giving audio acknowledgment to actions the user takes on the screen like clicking a button. Sound also helps your presentation to move along and convey different moods and tempo in different areas. Your choice of music and sound effects is probably the factor that will most impact the way your audience will experience your presentation.

Although most authoring applications allow you to include sound in your presentation, it is important to note here that it is illegal to use music from your favorite compact disc or something you taped from your favorite radio station in your presentation. Not to worry though; there are other alternatives. You can purchase royalty-free music on compact disk (CD).

You can use this music without fear of being sued to enhance your presentations. You may also want to add your own voice, to explain a particular concept. You can do this with a sound card and a microphone (for PC users) or use your Mac's built-in sound to digi-tize your voice for the presentation.

Video/Animation

Many firms are using computer animation and/or live video to demonstrate their design concepts to their clients. These clips can also be included in your multimedia presentation. Many CAD applications allow you to create animations, and these can be, if necessary, converted in DeBabelizer and brought into your presentation.

Many firms have realized the benefits of using three-dimensional modeling, rendering, and animation and, as a result, have dedicated applications to produce beautifully rendered 3D models which are then animated. Both the 3D models and the animations can be included in presentations.

You can also digitize video taken using a camcorder for your multimedia production, although you would need to purchase a video card to do so. Optionally, you can use stock video—video clips already digitized on a CD-ROM ready to use.

DESIGN AND INTERACTIVITY

Once you have addressed the issues in the planning phase, you can move on to the design phase. At this point, it is time to brainstorm and develop a storyboard. A storyboard is a step-by-step plan that will serve as the "blueprint" for your project. It must take into consideration three things: the content you wish to present, the links you want to establish, and the response you wish to illicit. Similar to a design program, it establishes a map for the presentation, showing how it will progress from one scene to another. You address the issues of flow and relationships of scenes with each other and with the audience. It is important to remember that these relationships, unlike in traditional presentations, are not necessarily linear. For example, a videotape goes from idea #1, to idea #2, to idea #3 in a linear fashion, simply going from one point to another. In a multimedia presentation, there can be multiple branches, links, "hot" buttons, and starting and ending points. In order to demonstrate all these relationships, you can use storyboards or flowcharts.

Another option is to use your project management software. It is just another way to help you understand the relationships within your project, and it is a tool that

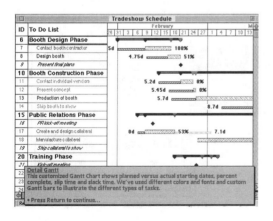

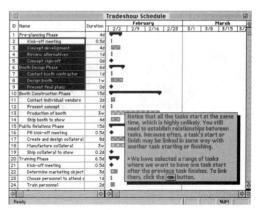

you are already familiar with. Using the project management software will allow you to keep track of all the components that make up your multimedia project. Video and audio clips, graphics, and sound files need to be tracked—the file name, format, location, and size.

Multimedia Database

While we are talking about different files, we should discuss the concept of a multimedia database. Just as you have flat file drawers for your hard copies of construction drawings, you can develop an electronic filing system to organize your graphics, sound, video, and other files into a multimedia database that you can use for other projects

An Adobe Fetch database containing some of C4 Studio's graphic files and a sound file.

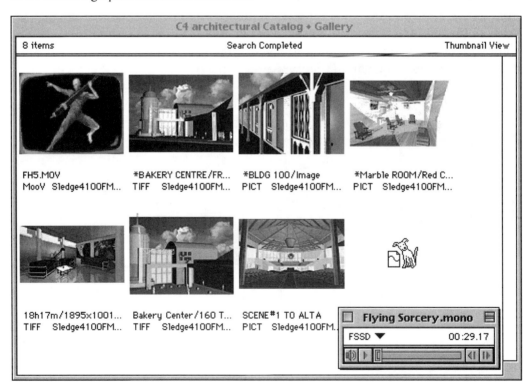

as you progress. A number of software applications exist that can help you with this task.

One specifically designed as a multimedia database is called Fetch, by Adobe. It saves your files in a library, and it will record important information that will allow you to easily retrieve the file at a later date; for example, tracking information such as file location; file size—how much space the file uses on your hard drive; file type—movie, sound, TIFF, PICT, and so on. Thumbnails, small pictures of your graphics, allow you to easily identify the needed file.

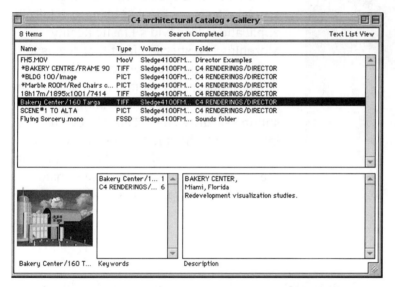

Using the Text List view, you can retrieve file information and any description you may have assigned to the file.

The movie file can be played within Fetch simply by double-clicking its thumbnail and clicking the start button on the bottom left.

Special Effects and Transitions

A transition is a special effect that takes place between scenes or frames. Transitions and special effects can add pizzazz and an air of professionalism to your presentation. The key is not to overdo it. Too many transitions can distract from and annoy an audience. They also slow

down the playback of your presentation. It is therefore important to find just the right balance between creating an interesting presentation and going overboard.

While many multimedia packages can do some limited special effects, most special effects are created using specialized applications like Avid's Elastic Reality. Morphing is a special effect that seems to make one image grow out of another, different image. An example can be seen on *Star Trek: Deep Space Nine* with the shape-shifting security chief. This can be an interesting technique to show something like a renovation, before and after, allowing the client to fully appreciate the transformation that has taken place.

PROTOTYPE

The next step is actually building a prototype. This is analogous to the building of a model, cardboard or computer, so you can visualize your project before moving on to actual construction. The purpose of the prototype is to work out any glitches with the linking and file formats, gain approval, and resolve any other issues before finalizing the presentation.

SOFTWARE SOLUTIONS

Multimedia is an industry buzzword for the '90s. You see it on equipment advertised as being "multimedia ready" or software touting its "multimedia capabilities." The result is a variety of software applications claiming the title even if they allow you to add only one of the components necessary to qualify as true multimedia. We will look at different applications that vary in price and "multimedi-ability." They all enable you to manipulate different media to varying degrees, and the major difference between them, besides the price, is how interactive they allow you to make your presentation; that is, the degree to which your audience or clients can participate in and interact with your presentation.

Microsoft PowerPoint

This application is Microsoft's entry into the multimedia arena. The interest in multimedia as an office necessity is evidenced by the inclusion of PowerPoint in its premier combination office product, Microsoft Office. Although PowerPoint is not strictly considered a true multimedia application, we will still take a look at its features because it is easy to use and is a good entry level candidate for your office.

PowerPoint utilizes a very familiar slide interface. Encompassed within the slide are the different types of media—text, clip art, and other graphics, as well as movies.

If you use MS Office, you can also import graphs or spreadsheets created in Excel or tables from MS Word directly into your presentation.

Among the other features, there are templates to assist you, any of which you can customize to give your presentation a polished look with a minimum of effort.

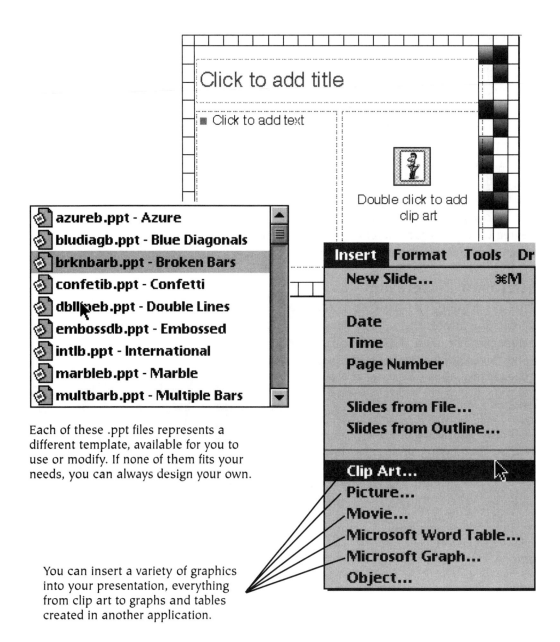

Click to add title

■ Click to add text

Double click to add clip art

azureb.ppt - Azure
bludiagb.ppt - Blue Diagonals
brknbarb.ppt - Broken Bars
confetib.ppt - Confetti
dbllineb.ppt - Double Lines
embossdb.ppt - Embossed
intlb.ppt - International
marbleb.ppt - Marble
multbarb.ppt - Multiple Bars

Insert   Format   Tools   Dr

New Slide...   ⌘M

Date
Time
Page Number

Slides from File...
Slides from Outline...

Clip Art...
Picture...
Movie...
Microsoft Word Table...
Microsoft Graph...
Object...

Each of these .ppt files represents a different template, available for you to use or modify. If none of them fits your needs, you can always design your own.

You can insert a variety of graphics into your presentation, everything from clip art to graphs and tables created in another application.

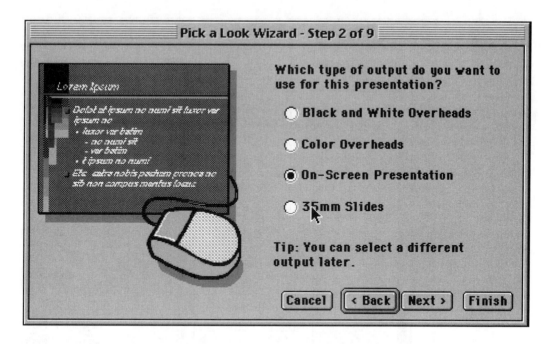

Which type of output do you want to use for this presentation?

○ **Black and White Overheads**

○ **Color Overheads**

◉ **On-Screen Presentation**

○ **35mm Slides**

Tip: You can select a different output later.

[Cancel] [< Back] [Next >] [Finish]

'Wizards' guide you through the making of your presentation. You are asked a series of questions, and your answers take you, step by step, through the creation of your presentation.

When preparing to do a presentation, you begin with an outline of key points you want to make with headers and subheaders, according to importance. You may create this outline in MS Word and import it into PowerPoint.

The outline is then portrayed on a slide, using the template you chose. Once your slides are completed, you can then add slide timing and transitions. Each slide can be set to stay on the screen a predetermined amount of time so you can vary the tempo of the presentation as needed for text or movies, in order to have sufficient time

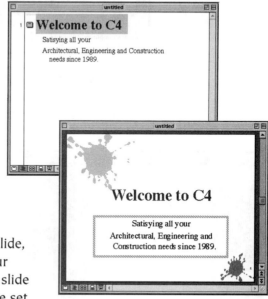

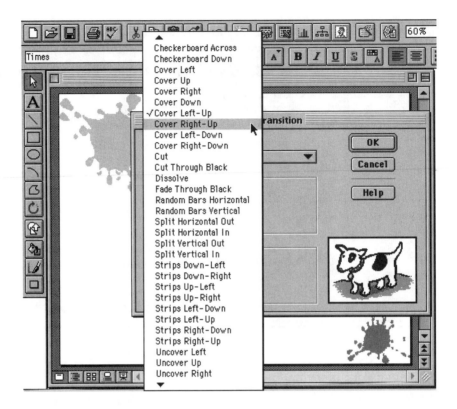

for viewing. The space containing the picture of the little dog in the bottom right of this figure gives you an opportunity to see an example of the transition before you apply it. Remember, the larger the graphics, the slower the transition, and the more transitions, the larger and slower the entire presentation. As you can see, there are many transitions to choose from. Remember not to get carried away!

You are also given an opportunity to create audience handouts and speaker notes with mini versions of the slides and space for taking notes.

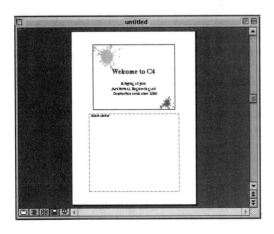

Macromedia Action!

Action! 1.0.4

Macromedia Action! is probably the best tool of the three applications discussed for creating multimedia presentations in your office when you consider all the pertinent factors: the learning curve, creative power, and ease of use. It has many of the same helpful features as PowerPoint, including an outliner for organization of key points and a template library for a professional and consistent look.

None of these tools, however, prevents you from creating your own customized presentation. You have micro control over all the objects on the screen. All the text and other objects can actually fly or transition onto and off of the screen. You can decide on:

- The **content** of each scene; the size and position of your files as you place them. It is set up in such a way that you can interchange files without having to redo the entire presentation.

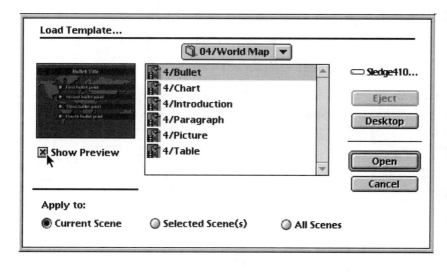

- **Links** between text or objects on the screen such that when you select the object or text, it takes you to another scene. (A scene in Action! is the equivalent of a slide in PowerPoint.)

- **Action** of the text or objects on entering the screen, during their stay, and on exiting the screen. Transitions and motion onto the screen are also controlled by this menu.

- **Duration** of the entire scene and the start time.

- Any **sound** attached to an object is controlled here. You cue up a sound (set its start time) and determine its duration of play.

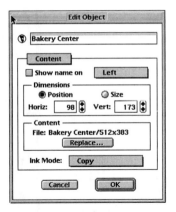
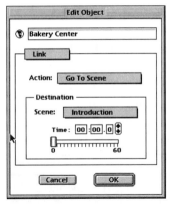

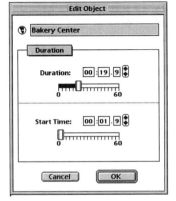
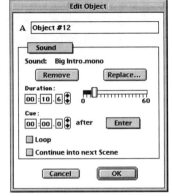

Macromedia Director

Director is probably the most powerful multimedia authoring application currently available. Many of the multimedia titles on the market today were created using Director. The titles are varied and illustrate well the versatility of the product. Many of the self-running software demos and tutorials included in today's software applications utilize Director. For the architect, Director offers true multimedia capability, and you can use it to create and distribute company and project titles.

Director is the most appropriate name for this application because the user is truly acting like a movie director controlling a cast. The members of the cast in this case are the graphics, sound, and movie items. Each cast member has a role to play over the time that the movie runs. That role is defined in the score. The sprites (copies of the cast members) in the score display information, frame by frame, about motion, sound, color, special effects, and scripts (programming).

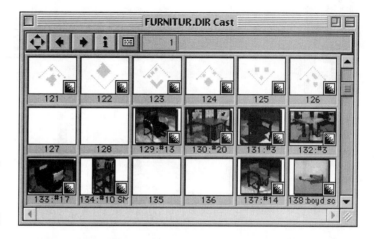

There are some familiar tools such as a paint window for editing graphics and a VCR-like interface for controlling the playback of the presentation. You can

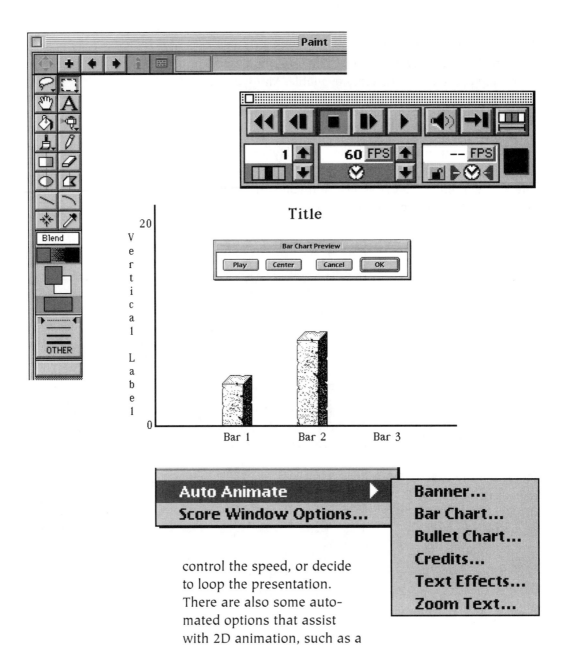

control the speed, or decide to loop the presentation. There are also some automated options that assist with 2D animation, such as a bar chart animation. You simply fill in the text for the axes and your own numbers.

Truth be told, however, Director is not an application that you can run out and purchase today and expect to use in your office tomorrow. The training curve is steep and requires a significant time commitment before becoming proficient.

To assist in the training effort, Macromedia offers two- and four-day live training sessions to which you can send an employee. CD training is also available to employees who may be interested in learning in their spare time, at their own pace.

The learning curve aside, we feel that with such a great premium being placed on presentation skills for gaining and keeping clients, Director is a product whose existence and capabilities you need to be aware of since it is impacting the profession now and will continue to do so as time goes on.

We had a call the other day from a firm interested in converting a PowerPoint presentation to a Director presentation so that it could be distributed on diskette to current and potential clients. The PowerPoint presentation was a 19 megabyte file. The problem is that a 19 MB file cannot fit on a floppy disk (1.44 MB). And though Director files can also be large, generally, you can create some really complex presentations that have a fairly small size. We were able to convert the file to a 2 MB Director file and achieve the same result as the original presentation. The file was then compressed to a 1 MB sea (self extracting archive) file that fit on a floppy disk for quick, inexpensive distribution.

Information can be distributed rather inexpensively electronically when compared to the costs associated with paper distribution. Electronic presentations may seem high-tech today but they will be common place tomorrow. Just look at the phenomenal growth of the Internet, the ultimate in electronic communications.

Architects can use Director presentations within our

practice to help achieve a number of tasks. You can create and use Director presentations as an introduction to your firm for clients. Before a client hires you, they like to know who you are. A presentation with sound and graphics showing past and current work, company philosophies, and personnel specialties can go a long way to making a client feel comfortable. These presentations can be upgraded to reflect new projects and can be used over and over again. New employees can also use these presentations as their introduction to your company.

PowerPoint file

The presentation that you compile of a particular project can be very useful to your client in securing investors and financing for the project. And clients may be willing to bear part or all of the cost involved in creating a presentation, especially if you point out that the presentation can be reused to market the project once it is completed and, in the case of something like a mall, can be made into a kiosk presentation directing people to points of interest within the mall once it is opened.

For distribution, Director creates what is called a projector file of your presentation. It is self-running and does not place any software requirements on your client to have Director or any other application in order to view your presentation. You simply double-click on the icon and your presentation is off and running.

Too big; can't fit

Smaller file can fit

Macromedia Authorware

Director's big brother, Macromedia's Authorware is an icon-based, multimedia authoring application primarily used for creating training applications, interactive courseware, interactive reference titles, kiosks, prototyping, and simulations. This user-friendly multimedia application includes ease-of-use enhancements designed for professionals like architects who want to create highly engaging, interactive marketing presentations without having to learn challenging programming or scripting languages.

The Most Powerful Authoring Environment For Interactive Information

We can also seamlessly integrate Director presentations in our Authorware presentations, making them more interactive than ever. Now we can open and use Director movies interactively in Authorware. Conversely, we can send Lingo commands from Authorware to Director movies and receive information back from Director on both Windows and Macintosh—truly a cross-platform multimedia solution.

Some of the features that make this multimedia authoring application most applicable for architects who have no formal training in this aspect of marketing presentations are as follows:

- Hyperintelligent Authoring: Complete hypermedia, including hypertext functionality has been added to Authorware allowing you to link to your word processing text, computer-generated or scanned-traditional graphics, sounds, and animation movies anywhere in your application.
- Conversion: Authorware can convert your multimedia marketing presentations from Macintosh to Windows as well as from Windows to the Macintosh.
- Online Help/Extensive Author Support: Becoming proficient in creating multimedia marketing presentations has now become easier than ever. Authorware's documentation has been enhanced to make creating interactive applications much easier. You can take

advantage of the comprehensive online help, revised tips and techniques, vastly improved descriptions of online variables and functions, and the first-ever Authorware Portfolio that explains more than 75 different, professional-quality models included for your use. In addition, the application is shipped with nearly 1,000 professional-quality custom buttons, sliders, panels, bullets, and more.

Even though Authorware has more user-friendly features than Director, it still requires an investment in time to become proficient and, with a price tag of $4,995, it may require a bank loan.

Authorware's Drag-and-Drop Authoring Interface

Multimedia marketing presentations are made easy through Authorware's object-oriented interface, which uses icons to define and control composition. You can create your presentations simply by placing icons on a flowline, eliminating the need for programming or scripting.

Display

Create or import text and graphics using a variety of special effects. It also provides access to an object-based graphics toolbox.

Motion

Move on-screen text, graphics, and digital movies from one point to another over a given amount of time or at a specified speed.

Erase

Use a wide variety of special effects to remove text, graphics, animations, and digital movies from the screen.

Wait

Pause the application until the end user clicks a button, presses a key, or times out.

Navigate

Use 10 different hyperlinks for navigating among frameworks, including links to specific pages, dynamic text searching, and custom links.

Framework

Create intricate navigation structures and hypermedia.

Decision

Invoke sequential, random, and conditional path branching capabilities.

Interaction

Control branching based on end user input. Here, users choose from various options including custom buttons, hot spots, and pull-down menus.

Calculation

Perform functions, manipulate variables, call external routines, and jump to other files or programs.

Map

Organize the logic flow and create a multilevel structure by combining related icons into one. You create design elements similar to an outline or flowchart.

Digital Movie

Import and play back digital video, including interactive Director Movies.

Sound

Import and play up to CD-quality audio, such as sound effects, music clips, and voice-overs.

Video

Play full-motion and still analog video sequences. Control start, end, freeze frames, playback speed, and repetition of sequences.

ICON PALETTE

Display
Motion
Erase
Wait
Navigate
Framework
Decision
Interaction
Calculation
Map
Digital Movie
Sound
Video

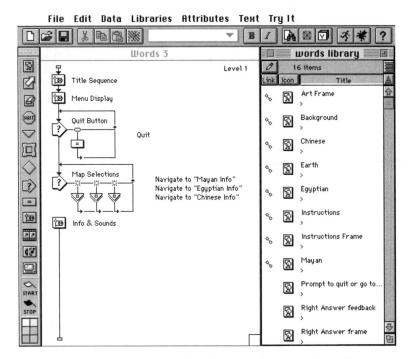

We built this presentation first by dragging the icons from the icon palette onto the flowline. For example, we first dragged the sound/narration icon onto the flowline, followed by the digital movie icon (containing the animation walk-through), the motion, pause, interaction, display (containing architectural renderings), pause, and finally the video icon (containing video interviews with principals of the firm). Next, we identified the icons by typing the title in the text field to the right of the icon while the icon was selected.

In order to assign the respective files to each icon on the flowline, we double-clicked (with the mouse) to access the appropriate dialog box. By double-clicking on the digital movie icon, this dialog appeared to set the parameters as well as load the animation files.

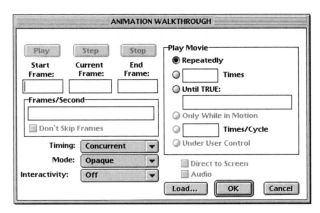

AN EDUCATOR'S PERSPECTIVE

The following interview is with Erick Valle, Professor of Architecture at the University of Miami.

CC: Curtis Charles
EV: Erick Valle

CC: One of the first things we want to look at is how architecture firms should be using multimedia for marketing.

EV: First of all, there are a number of different levels in which multimedia can be used for marketing. And of course all of these I'll be describing are in a digital format. The first example is one in which multimedia is used to create an interactive book, and within that book, you might include things like audio, video, text, and graphics. At the first level is this whole idea of making it small, and sending that small soundbit, that first impact. Some firms are beginning to put this onto floppy disks (and everybody has a floppy drive) and sending their work out on diskettes. These little snippets give an idea of the firm's impact, or the firm's decision. Today, I believe strongly that firms need to be developing an interactive CD-ROM. It will be the way many firms start marketing themselves.

CC: Do you anticipate architecture firms putting that together in-house?

EV: Ideally yes; realistically it's a different story. The truth is, architects always tend to be at the end of the path. I think architects should have full control of every aspect of design. Creating interactive multimedia should be done by the architect, as it should reflect the beliefs, the concepts, the ideas of that particular office. The ability of the architect to express him- or herself can only be done in-house, as architects are finding nowadays from designing everything from teaspoons to communities. This is just another aspect, another avenue of expression.

CC: In terms of architects doing that in-house, describe some of the things you are doing in your multimedia course to bring out this new breed of architects.

EV: There are two schools of thought. The first school of thought, in universities, is that you educate the student to program. This school says the applications are not out there, and the ones that are, do not understand how architects think. Therefore we should create our own applications, our own designs, and do our own programming

The other school of thought, which is the one I practice here, supports the idea one of creating and developing the skills based on the existing technology, showing the students the variety of technology that is available, not just design by architects but design used by many other professions. Students need to be educated in a way that gives them the exposure to the products that are out there and how they might actually use those products.

CC: How do you anticipate multimedia fitting in to tight deadlines schedules?

EV: Are we talking about creating an interactive CD-ROM for a project we are working on at the moment, or are we creating an interactive CD-ROM that talks about what the firm is doing? Those are two very different scenarios.

CC: Let's explore both.

EV: Many cities and communities are coming online, and coming online means more than just having a presence over the Internet, but actually bringing a certain level of understanding within all the departments. Eventually that will go on in the commission chambers. In lieu of all that is the idea of CDs becoming a form on which firms submit their work for an RFQ or RFP.

Now how long will it take? It depends on what you want to do with this technology and what you want to present.

CC: Are firms hiring a new kind of architecture graduate?

EV: Today we are hearing that firms aren't hiring architects who don't know how to use CAD. Soon that level will jump up another notch and they won't hire people who don't know how to do modeling, and the next level will be animation; and the next level will be that if they don't know how to do interactive CDs, "I'm sorry we can't hire you."

CC: What we are talking about, with the aid of computers, is having a complete architect who understands industrial design, visualization; who understands the environment. I don't want to make it seem like the computer is ruling the profession, but the computer is being used as an extremely intelligent tool. How are we going to convince the older architectural firms that this is a technology that needs to be embraced?

EV: I don't think we'll need to convince them. They'll be put in the position where they'll have to embrace it to be competitive with firms getting the jobs because they are able to convince their potential employers—the government or the private industry—that they are more versatile, more live, more online with technology.

CC: What do you see as the future for multimedia and architecture? How do you see smaller firms competing with this multimedia technology?

EV: I think there is a misperception that it is expensive, which is not necessarily the case. There are many entry levels to the technology. Many of the PCs out there have most of these capabilities built in. There are authoring tools that start at $99, for creating very simple slide shows that are multimedia. In the slide shows, you can have sound, you can have video integrated. You can get much more sophisticated and eventually have your own CD-ROM recorder and record your own CDs in-house. That technology has become inexpensive.

CC: Around $1,000.

EV: Three years ago, our school bought the same technology for $10,000; today, I could buy it for $1,000 or less. The same technology. Scanning and authoring tools are also going to be important and essential tools for marketing.

Delivery Media

DISTRIBUTION

O nce you have employed some of the great marketing techniques discussed previously in this book, you have to get them to your clients. The delivery medium is a choice that should have been made early in the planning stages of the project. If you don't do this, you could find yourself unable to show off your high-tech presentation. How you distribute your presentation is a decision driven by the client or audience to whom the presentation will be made. A number of questions need to be asked and answered about the audience prior to making these decisions.

- What equipment do they own? A personal computer, video, compact disk, nothing?
- What is the audience size? One person, a small group, or a packed auditorium.

- What kind of presentation? A short list, community/town meeting?
- Are you using U.S. mail, fax, or electronic mail on the Internet?
- Will you be there to present, or will your presentation have to speak for itself?
- Where is the presentation to be made? In the client's office, at a trade show, or somewhere else?
- Can you run the presentation off a laptop connected to a large monitor, TV, or overhead projector?

Knowing the answers to these questions will help you determine which of the many solutions presented in this book will best suit your needs. In turn, each situation will demand a different presentation medium be used in order to have the maximal impact. Paper, video, diskette, compact disks, the Internet, each can be used as the medium in which you make your presentation. It is important to keep in mind that one presentation can be adapted for use with multiple audiences, using different media to convey similar, reworked ideas. In this portion of the book, we will discuss these various distribution mediums and the types of presentations for which they are best suited. We will also look at the software and hardware utilized in preparation for distribution.

Media

Your choice of media is going to affect the way your audience experiences your presentation. Most of us are accustomed to presenting on paper, but somehow, multimedia just doesn't work well on paper so we have to look to other media. The first option that comes to mind is video, and while a multimedia title works much better in this medium, it is by no means the only option available to us. Other digital delivery media include diskettes, compact disks, laptops, kiosks, and, of course, the information super-highway, aka the Internet.

PAPER

Paper is still the medium used by most businesses for both inter- and intraoffice communication. It is the only medium that places no equipment requirements whatso-ever on the recipient, except maybe eyes. Coupled with the low cost of laser and color inkjet printers and plotters, you now have the ability to produce very striking paper documents in-house. To assist you in creating interesting pieces, mail-order paper houses like Paper Direct offer papers preprinted with color graphics for every business occasion.

For three-dimensional computer models and renderings, you can make prints of your work, on specially coated papers, to show clients. The special coating improves the brightness of the colors and overall image quality. Using the graphics packages referenced in the section on desktop publishing, you can create and print colorful site plans, design and lay out brochures, and even print business cards on your laser printer.

Many of the marketing techniques discussed in this forum, however, are not well suited for presentation on paper. While you may be able to print the images dis-played on your screen, sound, motion, and interactivity obviously cannot be reproduced on paper. Consider also the actual cost of printing and mailing associated with paper, and the fact that the paper itself has become increasingly expensive to purchase. Some of the other mediums compare very favorably price-wise. Digital distribution on diskette and other media offer some of the same benefits as paper without many of the drawbacks.

Above & left:
This is just an example of the many preprinted papers available from Paper Direct, one of the paper mail-order houses. The three here are trifolds for printing brochures. They are marked for easy folding, and they run through a laser printer.

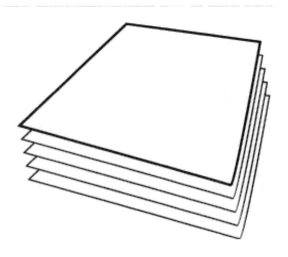

VIDEO

Video is a great way to communicate ideas accurately and concisely. Tasks like site analysis and animation walk-throughs are much easier to understand watching a videotape and listening to audio than reading a script or looking at still photos. Most people would rather look at a video describing a product or service than read the instruction manual. Videotape technology has progressed to the point that you can reasonably expect to find a unit in most offices. For all these reasons, it is important to explore the role video can play in the distribution cycle of your marketing materials.

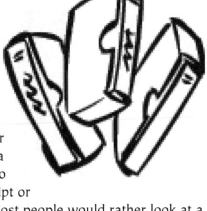

Many of the multimedia and animation applications we've discussed offer you the option to download to video. You need to use a device with a video-out jack to utilize this option. Apple's Macintosh has an entire product line—AV (audio-visual) Macs—that have the card built in, while for most PCs, you need to add an external device like Creative TV Coder from Creative Labs. This box allows you to send the video signal to any video display device, including your television. The device works by converting your computer's video signal into an NTSC or PAL signal, understood by your television. Some firms use this device to connect their large-screen television directly to their computer for presentations.

It is a cost-effective presentation solution because a large-screen monitor costs about twice as much as a large-screen television, the reason being that a computer monitor's screen resolution is much higher than that of a television's screen resolution. Connect your VCR between the TV and the computer, and you can record whatever appears on your screen—an animation or an Action or PowerPoint presentation. It is an inexpensive way to create video output from your computer. You may use the video cassette created as is, or take it to a professional studio for further editing.

With regard to the cost of the media itself, the tapes range in price from just over $1.00 to just under $3.00 for short-time increments—5-, 10-, 15-, and 30-minute cassettes. A videotape costs about $3.00 to mail in the United States so, as you can see, the prices are affordable when you consider the return—a big commission!

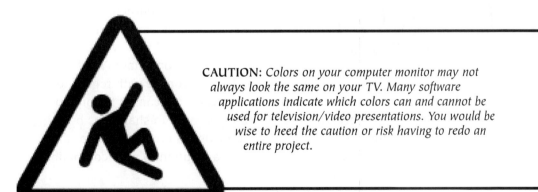

CAUTION: *Colors on your computer monitor may not always look the same on your TV. Many software applications indicate which colors can and cannot be used for television/video presentations. You would be wise to heed the caution or risk having to redo an entire project.*

DISKETTE

Between CAD and desktop publishing, almost all the documents produced in your office are created on your computer. If only your consultants, clients and co-workers could see these documents as they appear to you on your computer screen. With the possible exception of your CAD drawings, which you may be able to share with consultants who use the same CAD application as you, you will have to reduce your files to a hard copy; that is, put it on paper.

Currently, if you are able to share or exchange your documents electronically, it is only because you have agreed with your consultants to use the same application in order to facilitate the exchange. You have come to realize that digital documents are more efficient and cost-effective and you are willing to compromise for the sake of compatibility.

The problem with this particular compromise is that you may not be using the best software tool for *your* business even though it may be great for your consultant. While you may be able to compromise with regard to the CAD software you use, you certainly cannot accommodate everyone with whom you wish to share files by using the same software that they use. It obviously is not a practical solution. There is a solution to your compatibility problems.

Even though you have come to realize that digital documents are more cost-effective and efficient, until now, you have not been able to resolve all the compatibility issues. Do my clients use the same software I do? Do they have access to the same fonts? Do they even use the same computer!? The answer to all these questions can be found in a software application by Adobe called Acrobat.

Acrobat will help you provide electronic documents to your clients via its Portable Document Format (PDF). The really great thing is that you need not worry about what kind of computer your clients have or whether they have the program you used to create the original document The "portable" document can be viewed using Acrobat Reader, which can be freely distributed on the same disk as your document.

These electronic documents are not limited to black and white text either. You can include all the text and graphics options previously discussed, just as you created them. Color images can be viewed just as you created them, including complex blends and gradient fills. Imagine the possibilities! Instead of incurring the considerable cost associated with printing 1,000 four-color brochures, or printing on a low-resolution color inkjet printer, you can use Acrobat to make a PDF file and send it to your client on a diskette. Send as many or as few as you need to.

This gives your clients the freedom to explore your document at their leisure. You can enable them to print all or a portion of the document or none at all. Compared to the cost of distributing on paper, electronic distribution is more efficient and less expensive—not to mention the trees you would save.

Security Features

Architects are always concerned about maintaining and protecting the integrity of their architectural documents. Using the built-in security features of Acrobat, you have control over who can view and print your documents using password protection. This is more protection than you currently have for some of your printed documents. Unless you deliver the documents yourself, you don't

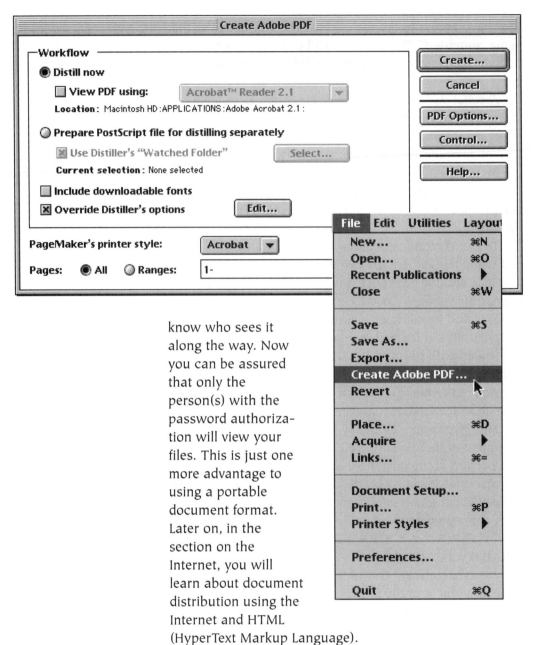

know who sees it along the way. Now you can be assured that only the person(s) with the password authorization will view your files. This is just one more advantage to using a portable document format. Later on, in the section on the Internet, you will learn about document distribution using the Internet and HTML (HyperText Markup Language).

You may be thinking "all this is well and good, but how many more applications do I have to buy?" Would

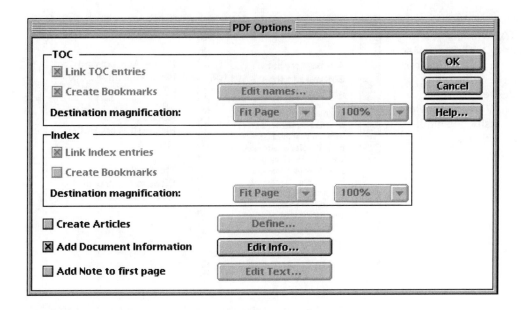

you believe one? Adobe's PageMaker not only performs page layout functions but includes two plug-ins to aid in the distribution of documents electronically.

The Acrobat and HTML plug-ins are just one more sign of the change in methods of document distribution. Traditionally, you had two ways to distribute your documents:

- printing on your laser printer, plotter, or other output device or,
- sending it to an outside printer.

Now, thanks to technological advances, you have a third, less-expensive option.

Once you've composed your document in PageMaker, you simply choose the option to create an Adobe PDF. You get a dialog box from which you can choose to include any special fonts you may have used, create a table of contents, bookmarks, and an index for easy location of the important information in your PDF.

Clicking on the QT and AVI text will link you to either a QuickTime (Mac users) or AVI (PC users) movie demonstrating the desired concepts. These AVI or QT movies could easily be animation walk-throughs of your project.

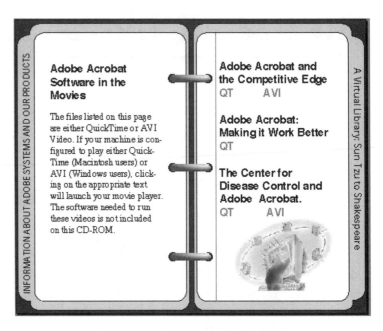

INFORMATION ABOUT ADOBE SYSTEMS AND OUR PRODUCTS

Adobe Acrobat Software in the Movies

The files listed on this page are either QuickTime or AVI Video. If your machine is configured to play either Quick-Time (Macintosh users) or AVI (Windows users), clicking on the appropriate text will launch your movie player. The software needed to run these videos is not included on this CD-ROM.

Adobe Acrobat and the Competitive Edge
QT   AVI

Adobe Acrobat: Making it Work Better
QT

The Center for Disease Control and Adobe Acrobat.
QT   AVI

A Virtual Library: Sun Tzu to Shakespeare

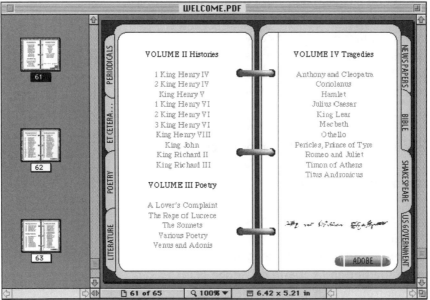

WELCOME.PDF

VOLUME II Histories

1 King Henry IV
2 King Henry IV
King Henry V
1 King Henry VI
2 King Henry VI
3 King Henry VI
King Henry VIII
King John
King Richard II
King Richard III

VOLUME III Poetry

A Lover's Complaint
The Rape of Lucrece
The Sonnets
Various Poetry
Venus and Adonis

VOLUME IV Tragedies

Anthony and Cleopatra
Coriolanus
Hamlet
Julius Caesar
King Lear
Macbeth
Othello
Pericles, Prince of Tyre
Romeo and Juliet
Timon of Athens
Titus Andronicus

ADOBE

61 of 65   100%   6.42 x 5.21 in

The Acrobat demo CD is full of PDF files created as examples including, as shown here, a listing of Shakespeare's works. The name of each work is a link that takes you to another PDF file of the work itself. The thumbnails of this PDF file are located to the left.

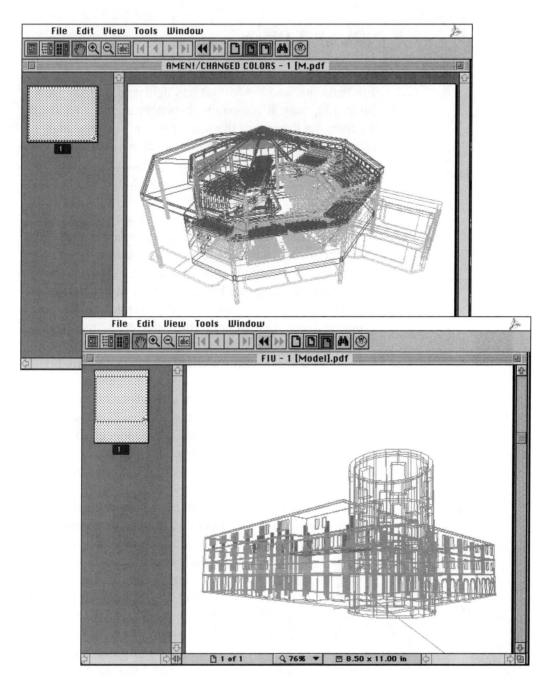

These two PDF files were created using a
modeling application's files using Acrobat.

COMPACT DISKS

Compact disks initially promised to replace recording on vinyl albums, and the format has delivered on that promise in a big way. It delivers high-quality sound on a sturdy medium not subject to the scratches and warping that plagued vinyl albums and is comparable in cost.

The advent of larger software applications and data-intensive multimedia titles led the way to the use of CD-ROM (Compact Disk Read-Only Memory) in the software arena. Many of you who are long-time users of AutoCAD remember when it came on just a few diskettes. You have watched in awe as it has grown to the point where the complexity of the application and all the new features require an alarming number of diskettes to be shuffled in, one after another, to install the latest version of the program. Now, instead of all those diskettes, just one CD-ROM is necessary. A single compact disk can hold up to 650 MB of data, the equivalent of 450 high-density diskettes!

With respect to multimedia, you'll recall from our previous discussion, that graphic images, digital audio and video files can eat up massive amounts of space. Remember the PowerPoint presentation that required almost 20 MB of space and, it didn't have any sound or video files!

Right about now, you might be asking yourself why you ever thought it was a good idea to market your services using multimedia if it was this space-intensive.

Lucky for you, there's an answer to that question! It's CD-R (Compact Disk-Recorder) for the desktop. Now your creativity is not limited by space considerations. You can create the presentation you want, for

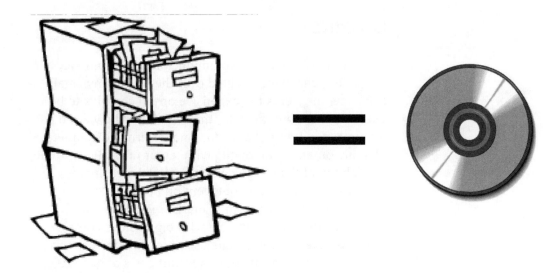

distribution on a compact disk that you "master." Master is the term used to describe the writing of data to a CD. CD-R is ideal for a user like you, who wants to create a small number of CDs. Prior to the availability of CD-R for the desktop, distribution of information on CD was not cost-effective unless you wanted to create a large number of them.

Starting at about $1,000, you can purchase a CD recorder for your desktop computer. It is relatively new technology and, as time goes by, and the technology improves, the price will decrease.

Some of you may think that the price may be more than you want to pay to create marketing CDs in house, but consider some of the other uses applicable to your office situation. If you use CAD to create your design and construction documents, CD-R would be a great way to archive your completed projects. Just think how many flat file drawers and storage closets you can do away with by storing your projects on CD. We've already established that the medium is sturdy and dependable. You could make two CD backups, kept in different places, and simply print documents as needed.

INTERNET

The Internet is all about communication. All your electronic files can be distributed over the Net. Many small firms feel the Net is too expensive or too complex to be useful to them but, in truth, the Net should be viewed as an equalizer. It is a chance for smaller firms to compete globally on an equal footing with larger firms. Prior to the availability of the Net to commercial activity, smaller businesses were simply outspent on projects. Small businesses do not have large marketing budgets and human resources to compete with big business on a financial level. The judicious use of technology can level the playing field. An Internet account costs about $20 a month. For that price, you can exchange mail and files and have an e-mail address. How much does your courier or FedEx account cost? The truth is, you can't afford *not* to be on the Net. You do not have to be an expert.

Initially, people primarily used the Internet to communicate via electronic mail (e-mail). It was too difficult to figure out how to do much else. Now, new software simplifies tasks and allows everyone to make better use of the many features of the Net. Eudora, an electronic mail software, for example, simplifies the task of sending and receiving mail and files. Some Internet-savvy firms al-

ready use the Net to transmit files between offices, to colleagues, consultants, and clients. It saves money when compared to traditional methods like express mail. The time saved can help you meet deadlines and avoid costly delays.

Earlier, we hinted at another way to use the Internet to disburse marketing information. The same graphics and text information you used in PageMaker 6.0 to lay out the company brochure can be converted to HTML format, the language of the Web, by a PageMaker plug-in. If you're counting, that makes three formats in which you can output information from PageMaker—traditional, Acrobat, and HTML—a truly versatile product!

Value-Added Plug-ins

The developers of the popular Web browser Netscape Navigator are working closely with software developers to introduce a series of plug-ins to add functionality to the Web. The plug-ins bring new media formats directly into the browser window. The user, your clients, will download and install the plug-in on their computers, and it will enable them to view the various media types on your site. We will look at a couple of the plug-ins that may be of use in the architectural arena. Many of them have been available only since November or December 1995.

Shockwave

Macromedia's plug-in—Shockwave—enables you to place your multimedia presentation on your Web page and have clients view the presentation online, complete with motion, sound, and interactivity. You can upload your "shocked" presentation to your Web site, giving your clients instantaneous access to the latest information. A multimedia presentation online gives you the potential to have a complete representation of your company in audio, video, and/or animation to the millions of users of the Internet, many of them potential clients.

Amber

Amber, from Adobe, allows you to view documents created in its popular portable document application, Acrobat. This plug-in allows architects to display our work on the Web, as a PDF file, to attract potential customers and to inform the public at large. The file retains its look and feel while giving you control, via its security features, of who can see or print the documents. It also maintains the characteristics of the PDF file; that is, bookmarks and links to other PDF files or even links to other sites on the Web.

Kiosks

Many of you may feel that you don't want to invest the time and money in some of these solutions for a one-time use. Well, there may be a way to avoid having that happen. Many owners, unless they're independently wealthy, have to borrow money to fund their project, either from a bank or some other investor(s). Investors do not like to sink money into projects without having any idea of what the outcome might be. For this reason, you may be able to convince the owner to pay for all or part of the cost associated with creating a presentation.

The other hook to sell a client on the idea of creating a presentation is the opportunity to use it in pre- and post-construction marketing, in TV commercials, videos, and kiosks. Developers of condominiums or other housing projects are notorious for trying to sell people homes that are not yet built. A rendered computer model can be a great selling tool, enticing buyers. They get to see exactly what they are buying. Kiosks like the ones in malls are computers with special touch-sensitive screens that allow

for interactivity without the use of a keyboard. That multimedia presentation you created can be adapted to sell the space in the mall, and then reworked to direct shoppers. People can use the kiosk to find their favorite stores, special events, or the food court, always a popular site.

Why have a home page on the Web? To answer that, let us consider and compare a Web page with another form of mass media advertising—the newspaper. A single business card-sized ad in your local newspaper

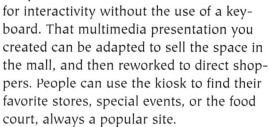

can cost hundreds of dollars weekly. This ad will reach only a finite number of people in the newspaper's local circulation area. If you have more money to spend, the next step up would be advertising in a national newspaper like *USA Today* or *The Wall Street Journal*. You then have to hope that people will be able to find your ad among all the others. Assuming they find your ad and want to contact you, they have to take another step to get in touch: either get to a telephone and make a call or write you.

In contrast, consider the Web home page scenario. A single page can potentially be seen by over 30 million Net surfers. People with an interest in architecture can do a search on the topic that will show them all the architecture pages. They can browse at their leisure. As with print advertisements, the more interesting your Web page, the more traffic you will attract. Once you've drawn the client in, you will take the opportunity to show color graphics depicting your company and the services or products you offer. Also included on your page can be a feedback form, giving the prospect the opportunity to communicate with you by electronic mail—immediately. Depending on your level of computer literacy and how much you can do yourself, all this will cost about $100 a month.

Neither scenario—the newspaper nor the Web page—includes the cost of initial development or regular update, both of which, with a background in design, you can do yourself.

In an effort to "cut to the chase," we will explain by example, some of the tasks you may want to perform on the Net. This how-to approach will allow you to actually achieve these tasks without having to read one of those really thick books on the Internet from cover to cover. The vast majority can be very confusing to the novice Web user. However, once you've gotten your feet wet, these texts can be an excellent resource. So, without further ado, let's dive in!

First, some terms:

HTTP stands for Hypertext Transfer Protocol. It is the set of rules by which your browser retrieves files from a server.

Web browser is the interface between the user and the World Wide Web. The names of some common browsers are Netscape, Mosaic, Cello, and Lynx.

HTML is the HyperText Markup Language. When you write a document in HTML, you specify not only the text of the document but also information about how the text should be formatted. The example to the left is a simple HTML document. Notice it begins with the HTML in tags— < >. All instructions are contained within these tags. <HTML> defines the start of the document while </HTML> defines the end of the document.

Pointers for striking Web pages:

1. Define a clear underlying theme, starting with your color scheme and continuing with your message and images.
2. Gather source material from your multimedia database—logos, resume, examples of your work, and the services you offer.
3. Make your page compelling and fun, to attract readers.

Congratulations! You've just created your first Web page using HTML. It wasn't that painful, was it? In order to view the result of the HTML program that we just wrote, we need to view it using a browser such as Netscape.

< HTML >

  < head >
    — defines the header section

  < title > Put Title Here
    — the text that appears here
      will be the title on the page

  < /title >
    — end title

  < /head >
    — end header section

  < body >
    — start body section

..the text of the body..
    — place the text of the body here

  < /body >
    — end body section

< /HTML >
    — end html document

A new product on the market, Adobe Pagemill, has eliminated the need to learn HTML altogether. It allows you to build and edit pages just as they would appear on the Web. It has an integrated browser so you can preview your page as you build it. The tools are similar to those found in your word processor. The text formatting—bold, header, body—can be easily accessed from a pull-down menu.

Linking text or graphics to other HTML pages has never been easier. You can choose to use different colors for your background or you can use a graphic. Pagemill will tile the graphic and create the background for you. It even offers an easy-to-create form feature with different types of buttons. You can create a scroll bar or use radio buttons in your form. A pasteboard allows you to keep graphics close at hand for placement in the document. It took us less than half an hour to create our own home page using Pagemill right out of the box, compared to the six or so hours we spent trying to get the hang of creating HTML in a plain text editor. You can be up and running just as quickly. This is a great product, and it retails for less than $100.

Style	Format	Wir
Plain	⇧⌘P	
✓Bold	⌘B	
Italic	⌘I	
Teletype	⇧⌘T	
Strong	⇧⌘S	
Emphasis	⇧⌘E	
Citation	⇧⌘C	
Sample	⇧⌘A	
Keyboard	⇧⌘K	
Code	⇧⌘O	
Variable	⇧⌘U	
Raw HTML	⇧⌘H	

Although Adobe PageMill was one of the first products to present users with drag-and-drop tools for creating WEB pages, Macromedia and Microsoft have weighed in with similar products.

An easy-to-use
icon-based menu.

The Attributes Inspector allows you to easily
adjust text, image, and page parameters.

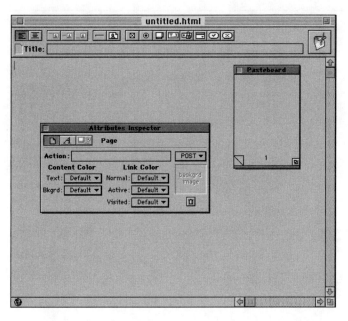

The pasteboard stores images so you
don't have to search for each one.

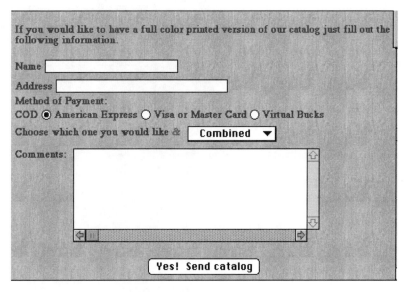

The forms offer a variety of options—radio buttons,
pull-down selection, and message boxes with scroll bars.

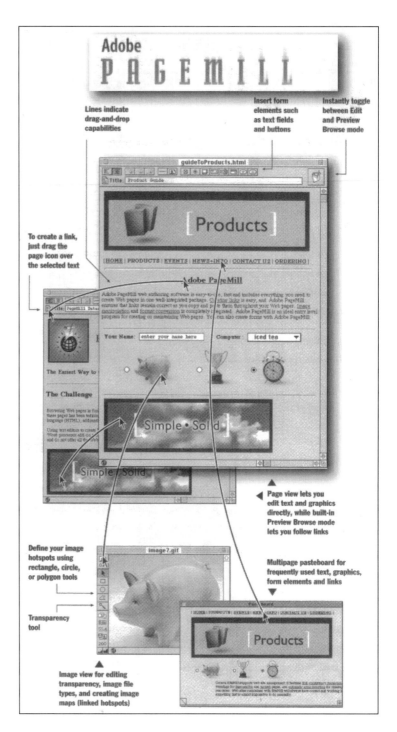

In order to create links between your firm's Web pages, simply drag a page icon from one document and drop it into another. Similarly, if you need to place graphics in your Web pages, just copy and paste graphics from any drawing program. Pagemill automatically converts these graphics into the appropriate file format for the Internet.

DESKTOP VIDEO CONFERENCING

First we communicated through signals, then word of mouth; eventually, the telegraph gained popularity, and it was soon followed by the telephone. In the twentieth century and the age of computers, we are no longer satisfied with just hearing those we communicate with. We have all seen the AT&T videophone ads featuring small, TV-like screens capturing not only the conversations between one person and another but their moving images as well. The wave of technology that is making this possible is video conferencing, a communication device that has steadily been gaining acceptance as an indispensable, real-time communication tool for marketing to clients and collaborating with associates.

What Is Video Conferencing

Video conferencing is not simply what its name implies, a conference call with video capabilities. Rather, video conferencing involves video, audio, and data transmissions and interaction among persons at different sites, all in real time. It can be thought of as a mix between a television, a phone and, most important, a computer terminal. This technology allows us to send, view, and interact with each other's design documents, spreadsheets, databases, images, text documents, and scores of other software applications. The key to video conferencing is this interaction or collaboration between the parties exchanging visual, audio, and computer signals. There are many advantages for architects who must collaborate with many other consultants to bring a client's project to fruition. There are the telephone calls, voice mail messages, fax, express mail, airplane travel, all so we can sit down together for an hour or two to finalize design and construction decisions. Think of the time and money you could save if you were able to video conference and get each other's feedback while everyone looks at the same file.

Requirements for Video Conferencing

Since optimal use of video conferencing entails video, audio, and data transfers, a VC (video conferencing) computer system should have an audio card to capture sound and a video card with enough speed and memory to process the real-time movements of any visual images being shown, so that it can process and download information quickly at more than one site simultaneously.

The next necessity for video conferencing is the connection between the computers or sites themselves. Since computers hook up to one another via telephones lines, modems are required. Using plain old telephone lines (POTS) and a product like Creative Labs' ShareVision, your firm can set up an inexpensive video conferencing system.

Another solution uses faster ISDN (Integrated Services Digital Networks) lines. This is a better solution for those firms that anticipate using video conferencing as a regular means of communicating with clients and consultants. Intel ProShare is one such product that takes advantage of ISDN's technology.

Let's look at a typical office scenario to illustrate how you can use video conferencing to win that commission.

Creative Labs' ShareVision video conferencing solution over POTS.

9:30 A.M.:

The contract is on the line. You just found out the proposal is due at 2:00 P.M. Your resources are spread throughout the country.

9:32 A.M.:

Your mission? Stay one step ahead of the competition, deliver the best proposal, and win the job. Your secret weapon? Your video conferencing system.

9:46 A.M.:

From accounting in the Minneapolis office: "These figures look great! Make these revisions and we're ready to roll."

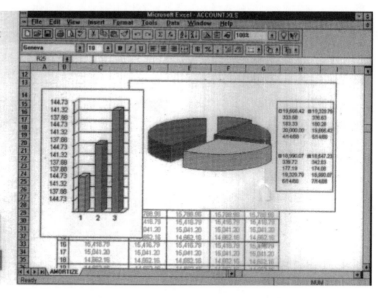

10:27 A.M.:

From the bank in Seattle: "Everything looks in order. Here's a table of the current financing rates we can lock in."

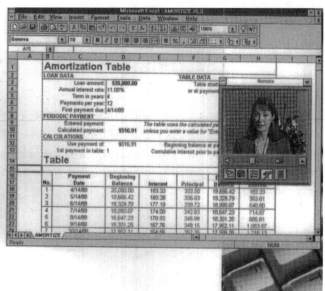

"Everything looks in order. Here's a table of the current financing rates we can lock in...!"

11:07 A.M.:

From the attorneys downtown: "Looks solid, as long as you make these minor changes to the contract!"

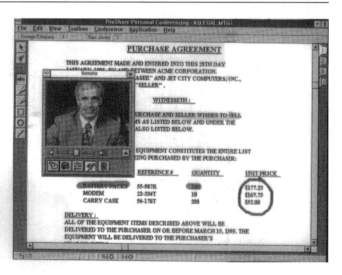

"Looks solid, as long as you make these minor changes to the contract...!"

11:37 A.M.:

From the engineer in Los Angeles: "We just finished the final schematics; let's take a look at the CAD files."

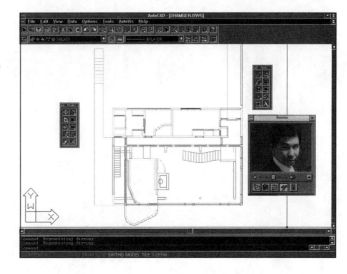

"We just finalized the schematics; let's take a look at the CAD files...!"

11:45 A.M.:

From the board of directors in the London office: "Everyone agrees the proposal is comprehensive, Dave. Great work—it's a go!"

Sources Consulted:

http://www.connors/know.html
http://www.interacess.com/sylver/proshare.html
http://www.totw.com/vvover.htm
http://www.ilios.eng.monash.edu.au/vbts/pamphlet.html
http://www.fiddle.ee.vt.edu/suceed/vj
http://www.bitscout.com/FAQBS
http://www.calpoly.edu/

Multimedia Marketing in Action

Chapter 7

This interview was conducted by author Curtis Charles with two members of the Marketing Department for an award-winning, multidisciplinary architecture/engineering firm in Miami, Bermello, Ajamil & Partners. Participating were Rebecca D. Martin, director of marketing, and Michael Simmons, manager of multimedia services.

Curtis: Let's discuss how Bermello, Ajamil & Partners uses multimedia as a marketing tool.

Rebecca: First we have to define what we call multimedia.

Mike: What we do it is not true multimedia. Currently our typical presentation uses Microsoft PowerPoint as a visual aid to the speakers.

Rebecca: We use PowerPoint both in pursuing projects, and after we are awarded the work. It can be a valuable tool. For example, if someone wanted a new office building or wanted to expand a cruise terminal, it is extremely convenient to visually articulate what-if scenarios, show the footprint of the existing building, and different ways it can be developed.

Mike: Elevational massing and similar display techniques can be accomplished with simple graphic tools in multimedia programs. A step up from that is incorporating sound and/or video. Generally, we work with TV graphics. You can go to these other items, but often time doesn't permit.

Rebecca: Or the budget. When the firm is pursuing a project, the probability of getting it must be balanced with the expense of using these tools and staff time. If you are not confident of the outcome, or if the project is not a very large one, you do not want to "invest the whole store." Once the firm has the project, the client may want to see what-if scenarios, and be willing to bear the expense. Then there are other tools available, including 3D. We would invest in modeling or animation when appropriate, not for every potential project. We recently did an animation segment for a short-listing presentation, but we've been able to use it for other things, too.

Curtis: Getting back to 2D, to PowerPoint presentations, how do you do the type of analysis that Rebecca is talking about, the what-if scenarios?

Mike: They're done in basically plan view and the elevational view, using different blocks of color for highlighting and annotation. We create 2D graphics in illustration packages such as Adobe Illustrator, Corel Draw or Photoshop, then import the figures into PowerPoint. That way, they can also be brought into print materials we produce.

Curtis: What has client response been to your use of presentations done in PowerPoint?

Rebecca: Very positive. PowerPoint adds movement to a presentation. For a long time, B&A was the only firm doing PowerPoint presentations, and clients (or prospective clients) were dazzled. They definitely saw us as high-tech, on the front end of things. But now others have begun using PowerPoint, either because they've purchased it or used outside consultants. It is getting to be now what slides used to be.

Curtis: How do you compare the PowerPoint presentation to traditional 24 x 36 boards?

Rebecca: For any presentation, the presenter makes the topic come alive, and makes it successful. Using any kind of electronic medium is no substitute for speaking skills. A really skilled presenter can control the room equally well using boards or PowerPoint.

Mike: A number of electronic presentation programs are available, many costing about $100. A major advantage any electronic program has over boards is fluidity and flexibility: last-minute corrections can be made at, literally, the last minute. If you're using boards that require an hour or more to plot, you're not going to be making a correction as you sit in the lobby waiting. Your ability to incorporate changes on the fly can make or break a presentation.

Curtis: How have you used video in presentations?

Rebecca: Video can, as you know, be combined into a PowerPoint presentation. All it takes is money and time. Video can be a strong selling tool; it can grab and hold audience interest. Video also captures aspects that straight PowerPoint cannot. For example, our firm had a video crew at the Homestead Motorsports Complex, which we designed, for the Busch Grand National Finale race. You will never be able to convey with something like PowerPoint the heart-pounding excitement of being at a racetrack on race day. Sometimes, one technique is more appropriate than the other.

Curtis: I am interested in video because elsewhere in this book we talk about architects using video as a marketing tool. We wanted to present three solutions:

1. a Targa board and a Pentium for a desktop solution
2. a nonlinear editing system in-house, like Avid or Media100
3. the outsourcing solution

Which of those solutions do you see for your company?

Rebecca: We expect to continue using a video production company for now. The firm will invest in some of the other technologies that have a more direct application to designing and CAD systems, rather than investing in video production in-house now.

Mike: The lowest-end video production set is $10,000. And you must have somebody trained properly; editing video and doing it right on a real editing system isn't like running your VCR at home.

Rebecca: We invest in the technology that gives our clients what they want. For example, with Macromedia Director, we can show flow and circulation for a cruise terminal design, illustrating how increasing the number of ticket counters can avoid logjams—which translate into unhappy cruise passengers. That's very valuable to us and to our clients.

Curtis: Let's suppose a video costs you $4,000 or $5,000, and you do three or four videos a year. You would be over the cost of a nonlinear system. Even considering this, it's not worth it to you to buy a system?

Rebecca: Experience tells us we wouldn't produce four videos a year, so for the other $15,000 I'd rather buy a program and training for staff who could do modeling, animation, and simulation every day of the year. Offering a capability that has more to do directly with design and how design looks and how it affects our clients is a much better investment and competitive advantage for us than to buy video capability. It is old technology—useful but old. We want to stay out here in front.

Curtis: Your main use of multimedia is in presentations. How do you budget that in getting a project?

Rebecca: We invest in the presentation, depending on the project. For example, it may be important to show phasing of construction, to give a visual understanding of the need to block off and reroute traffic at different stages of a project. These things are useful for the client to know, and it's important for the client to understand that we've already thought it out. In this case, you may call PowerPoint a low-level presentation tool, but for us it was the best choice.

Curtis: PowerPoint is a great tool to show things like phasing. I know the project you describe. All the clients wanted to see was how you were going to solve their problems; the first thing that came to my mind was a multimedia presentation showing how this work was going to be completed.

Rebecca: What clients want to know is, "How is this going to affect me? How much is it going to cost? What does it look like?" If your firm has been short-listed, presumably the client thinks you have the qualifications. So at the short-listing phase, the client wants to know, "What are you going to do for me on this project, and how?"

Curtis: Can you elaborate on investing more in design technologies?

Mike: Basically, the firm is always looking for a better medium, one offering more function. Right now we're evaluating other programs, other platforms so we can produce better presentations. The newest version of PowerPoint could be an option, with its inclusion of some basic animation features. We're still investigating.

Rebecca: We are looking at packages that can be used specifically for particular project types, like airports. The company has made the decision to allot a large portion of one person's time to searching out and evaluating these technologies.

Curtis: What about Macromedia Authorware? Have you looked at Authorware as a marketing/training tool?

Mike: We have Macromedia Authorware in-house. I like it a lot. I think it has a lot of advantages for creating walk-throughs where you have a lot of information to be communicated.

Curtis: Many architects were forced to get into CAD in the '80s, at least partially because CAD indirectly became a marketing tool. We were competing with each other based on CAD technology for clients. Is this the same direction that B&A is headed with respect to advanced technology, that it could also be used as a marketing tool?

Mike: Well, we use the fact that we are a completely Autodesk AutoCAD-based company as a marketing tool.

Rebecca: We have approximately 160 workstations, all networked. We use Autodesk AutoCAD Release 12 for DOS and also Release 13 for Windows. Not many clients are upgraded to 13 yet.

Mike: We have to go with what our clients use, and demand from our client base helps justify the cost of new software.

Curtis: Since B&A was one of the first firms in the area using PowerPoint, do you feel like a pioneer in terms of what other firms in Miami follow?

Rebecca: The goal of our principals is to stay on the leading edge of technology. We have built a reputation for applying technology to design as well as presentation in the best, most cost-effective way, and we want to maintain that. We have made a corporate decision to do that.

Curtis: The Internet. What's your take on how B&A intends to use the Internet as a marketing tool or as a resource?

Mike: Right now it's primarily a resource. I don't feel it will be a key marketing tool for architects and engineers for the next three or four years.

Rebecca: However, currently the ability to say we are Internet-equipped, proficient, and active is in itself a marketing tool.

Mike: How you use it now and how you intend to use it is directly relative to who is on the Internet, something that is forecastable. Estimates are that in three to four years, 80 to 90 percent of companies will have an Internet presence or an account.

Curtis: If you feel it will be four years before you can use the Net as a marketing tool, why have a page there now?

Rebecca: The Internet now is essentially a consumer market; generally, we do business-to-business marketing. However, the same types of activities we undertake to make ourselves known to consumers at large through community activities and press releases, we would also do on the Internet. For example, on the World Wide Web page we're building, we have press releases about design awards we won recently. In addition, there are governmental and institutional people on the Net who may be interested in contacting an architect or an engineer.

Curtis: What about the other things we do on the Internet? We know everybody uses it for mail, but do you use it for remote collaboration, exchanging files, and so on?

Mike: Yes, we do, on a regular basis. We now have five in-house Internet accounts. Each major department has its own account. Architecture uses its account to transfer files with consultants and clients all the time. It has saved days of transfer time, cross-country, across the world. In 15 minutes, the file is there, and somebody can be saying, "Yes I like this," or "No, I don't like that."

Rebecca: We're also using it to beat time zones and work around the clock. For example, we're the designer for a project in Spain. In the evening, we can electronically send files to our joint venture partner firm in Spain, which is doing construction documents. By noon the next day, we can have their files back here.

Mike: It doesn't even have to be an international project for us to benefit. We had a project with such a short time line that client responses were needed on daily changes.

Curtis: So what was the solution?

Mike: The solution was the Internet. The project was on schedule only because that resource exists.

Curtis: What about government agencies that we have to go through for permits? Are the agencies adapting to the new technology?

Mike: The large government agencies were on the Internet long before any of us were. For example, you can submit applications for copyright or patents electronically over the Internet. I foresee that government agencies will eventually develop that same technology for permitting. Metro-Dade County already has a dial-up BBS you can use to find project notices, meeting schedules, new announcements, and so on. Our planning department now conducts maybe 90 percent of its research on the Internet. Many new items being produced are already on the Net. For example, the popular aerial maps are available, and many you can download free of charge.

Rebecca: For me, there's no substitute for opening the big map and poring over it. Maybe I'm old-fashioned.

Mike: It's just a different school—I would much rather look at it in Photoshop and blow it up 400 percent (laugh) and get it even bigger than it comes printed.

Curtis: Exactly! You may just come from different schools. But I want to present the idea in this book to smaller firms that using electronic marketing techniques is not out of their reach.

Mike: I believe that for the $20 or $30 a month an Internet account costs, it is an investment a small firm can make. It gives you the ability to interact with other people without being in their office, and that's invaluable.

Rebecca: Even if a firm cannot afford to invest in all these things right now, there's a huge opportunity cost associated with not even being aware of them. And even if you have to buy the service outside, whether it is modeling or a shared Internet account, you have to be aware of it and aware of the opportunities. If you're not, you're going to lose.

Mike: For example, using the wireframe view in your 3D computer models as a skeleton for rendering saves time, and time is money. I can tell you that I need a south-side view instead of a north-side view coming in at a certain angle, and you can rotate the computer model in a few minutes, as opposed to the hours it would take to generate another hand-drawn perspective. That's just money back into your pocket.

Curtis: As we conclude, where do you see all this technology fitting into the practice?

Mike: It's a tool. Use it properly and you'll benefit from it. You don't use a screwdriver to put a nail in the wall—it's the same thing with the Internet or with multimedia applications. If you use the right tool at the right time, you're going to get the best product.

Rebecca: As leaders in the architecture and engineering field, we have to be aware of and competent with all the tools, including new technologies, and know when and how to use them properly.

Curtis: What is your advice to smaller firms as far as this technology is concerned?

Rebecca: Be aware of it and acquire it as appropriate and as you're able to. Additionally, there are enough service providers that you don't have to make your own investment; you can make alliances or use an outside provider.

Mike: For instance, someone in your class asked about doing stationary and graphic pieces. You don't have to hire a full-time artist. Hire a freelance artist or small advertising firm to produce these pieces for you. They'll do a better job than you could, you don't have the over-head of a full-time staff member, and it will save you time. You can turn the basic materials over to that person, then apply your time to other, revenue-producing projects.

Rebecca: It's particularly important for small firms to do what they do best. Use outside help for those things you don't do as well. If I pay an outside provider $50 an hour to accomplish something I don't do very well anyway, and it frees me up to work on projects for which I earn $100 an hour, I win.

Index

About the CD-ROM

What is on the CD-ROM?

The CD-ROM accompanying *Multimedia Marketing for Design Firms* contains:
- A presentation of sample analytical renderings and animation
- Demo software

Demo software included:

Action, Acrobat, After Effects (Mac), Archicad (Windows), Authorware, Dimensions (Mac), Director, Form-Z, Framemaker, FreeHand, Illustrator (Mac), PageMaker, PageMill (Mac), Persuasion, Photoshop, Premiere, Streamline, Studio Pro Blitz (PowerMac), TreePro (PowerMac)

Both Windows and Macintosh versions of demo software are provided on the CD-ROM unless otherwise indicated.

Note: Contact software vendor for latest information about available platforms for full working versions.

Demo versions are save-disabled or have limited functionality.

This CD-ROM is Macintosh and Windows compatible.

System Requirements

1. Presentation of Sample Images

   Windows:
   386/33 Mhz or higher PC compatible computer, 8+ MB RAM, Windows (3.1+, NT, 95), 256 color monitor, and CD-ROM drive

   Macintosh:
   68020 processor or greater, 8+ MB RAM, System 7.0+, 256 color monitor, and CD-ROM drive

2. Demo Software
   Please refer to the readme file in each software directory or folder for information about system requirements.

Installing and Running the Software

1. Presentation

   Windows:
   To view the presentation of sample analytical renderings choose File, Run from the menu bar in Program Manager and type (replacing X with the letter of your CD-ROM drive):
   X:\EXAMPLES\START.EXE

   You can also open the Examples directory in File Manager and double click on the start.exe file.

   Macintosh:
   To view the presentation of sample images and animation movies, double click on the **start here** icon in the **Presentation of Sample Images** folder located in the **Examples** folder.

2. Demo Software

Windows Installation:

To run the program and setup executable files choose File, Run in Program Manager and select Browse. Select the correct letter for your CD-ROM drive. Open the directory of the program you want to use and select the program or setup file. See list below for names of program and setup files for each program.

For example, to launch the **Archicad** program, choose File, Run in Program Manager and select Browse. Select the correct letter for your CD-ROM drive. Double click on **3DVISUAL** and double click on **ARCHICAD**. Select ARCHICAD.EXE and click OK. The following should appear (replace X with the letter of your CD-ROM drive): **X:\3DVISUAL\ARCHICAD\ARCHICAD.EXE**

Click OK and follow the directions on the screen.

See right hand column for location of program, setup, and readme files.

DIRECTORY	PROGRAM / SETUP
README.TXT	
3DVISUAL	
ARCHICAD	\archicad.exe
	\read_me.wri
RZ_DEMO	\rz_demo.exe
COMGRAPH	
FREEHAND	\f50bdemo.exe
	\readme.txt
STRMLINE	\slsetup.exe
	\readmesl.wri
DELIVERY	
ACROBAT	\acroread.exe
	\readme_r.txt
DESKPUBL	
FRAMEMAK	\disk1\setup.exe
	\disk1\readme.txt
PAGEMAKR	\setup.exe
	\readme.wri
DESKVIDE	
PREMIERE	\disk1\setup.exe
EXAMPLES	\start.exe
IMAGEEDI	
PHOTOSHP	\disk1\setup.exe
MULTIMED	
AW3	\aware3wm.exe
	\readme.wri
DIRECTOR	\director.exe
PRESENTA	
ACTION	\setup.exe
	\readme.wri
INFOCUS	
PERSUASN	\pr3.exe
	\read_1st.wri
	\readme.txt

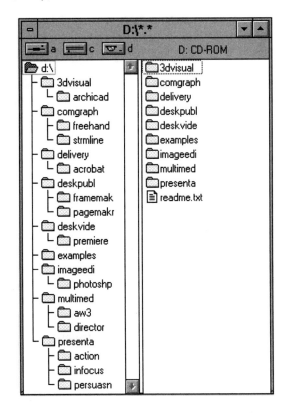

Windows Demo Software Name/Version:

Archicad 4.55, Form-Z RZ 2.8, FreeHand 5.0, Streamline 3.0, Acrobat 2.1, FrameMaker 5.0, PageMaker 6.0, Premiere 4.01, Photoshop 3.05, Authorware 3.0, Director 4.0, Action 3.0, Persuasion 3.0

Macintosh Installation:
Double click on the program or installation icon that appears in each software folder. Some demo programs can be run off the CD-ROM and others need to be installed onto your computer's hard drive.

README.TXT
3D Visualization
    form-Z RZ Demo (2.8)
    Studio Pro Blitz Demo (1.75)
        (Demo version—PowerMac only)
        (Copy folder to desktop before installation)
    TreePro (3.0)
        (Demo version—PowerMac only)
Communication Graphics
    FreeHand (5.5)
    Adobe Dimensions 2.0 Tryout
    Adobe Illustrator 6.0 Tryout
    Adobe Streamline 3.1 Tryout
Delivery
    Acrobat Reader Install (2.1)
Desktop Publishing
    Framemaker 5.0 Tryout
    Adobe PageMaker 6.0 Tryout
Desktop Video
    Adobe After Effects 3.0 Tryout
    Adobe Premiere 4.0.1. Tryout
Examples
    Start
Image Editing
    Adobe Photoshop 3.0.5 Tryout
Internet
    PageMill 1.0 Tryout
Multimedia
    Authorware (3.0)
    Director (4.0)
Presentation
    Action (1.0)
    In Focus (Use Photoshop to view images)
    Adobe Persuasion (3.0)

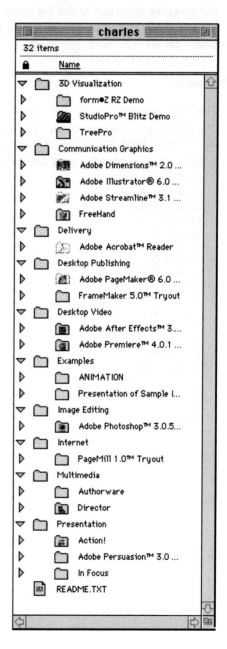

Technical Support

If you have problems with installation or your CD-ROM is defective, please contact John Wiley & Sons, Inc., Technical Support at 212-850-6194, Monday–Friday, 9am–4pm EST.

For questions about how to use the demo software contact the software vendor.

To place orders for additional copies of this book or to request information about other Wiley products, please call 800-879-4539.

Credits

The presentation on the CD-ROM was created with Macromedia Director 5.0.

Images in this presentation were created by:

C4 Studio
Manuel H. Ayala
Jose M. Bofill
Karen M. Brown
Carolin Butz
Gustavo Cardon
Simone Christian
Andrew Cogar
Charles B. Curtis
James B. Dougherty
Eugene Hernandez
Chris Herr
Nicholas Johnson
Brion Kean
Ramon Lastra
Rodrigo Reyes
Rafael Tapanes
Douglas West
Michael Wilson

ADOBE SYSTEMS INCORPORATED
MINIMUM TERMS OF END USER AGREEMENTS

MACROMEDIA
END-USER LICENSE AGREEMENT

PLEASE READ THIS DOCUMENT CAREFULLY BEFORE BREAKING THE SEAL ON THE MEDIA PACK-AGE. THIS AGREEMENT LICENSES THE ENCLOSED SOFTWARE TO YOU AND CONTAINS WAR-RANTY AND LIABILITY DISCLAIMERS. BY BREAKING THE SEAL ON THE MEDIA ENVELOPE, YOU ARE CONFIRMING YOUR ACCEPTANCE OF THE SOFTWARE AND AGREEING TO BECOME BOUND BY THE TERMS OF THIS AGREEMENT. IF YOU DO NOT WISH TO DO SO, DO NOT BREAK THE SEAL. INSTEAD, PROMPTLY RETURN THE ENTIRE PACKAGE, INCLUDING THE UNOPENED MEDIA PACK-AGE, TO THE PLACE WHERE YOU OBTAINED IT, FOR A FULL REFUND.

1. Definitions

(a) "Macromedia® Software" means the software program included in the enclosed package, and all related updates supplied by Macromedia.

(b) "Macromedia Product" means the Macromedia Software and the related documentation and models and multimedia content (such as animation, sound and graphics), and all related updates supplied by Macromedia.

2. License. This Agreement allows you to:

(a) Use the Macromedia Software on a single computer.

(b) Make one copy of the Macromedia Software in machine-readable form solely for backup purposes. You must reproduce on any such copy all copyright notices and any other proprietary legends on the original copy of the Macromedia Software.

(c) Certain Macromedia Software is licensed with additional rights as set forth in the Supplementary Rights Addendum that may be included in the package for this Macromedia Product.

3. Supplementary Licenses

Certain rights are not granted under this Agreement, but may be available under a separate agreement. If you would like to enter into a Site or Network License, please contact Macromedia.

4. Restrictions

You may not make or distribute copies of the Macromedia Product, or electronically transfer the Macromedia Software from one computer to another or over a network. You may not decompile, reverse engineer, disassemble, or otherwise reduce the Macromedia Software to a human-perceivable form. You may not modify, rent, resell for profit, distribute or create derivative works based upon the Macromedia Software or any part thereof. You will not export or reexport, directly or indirectly, the Macromedia Product into any country prohibited by the United States Export Administration Act and the regulations thereunder.

5. Ownership

The foregoing license gives you limited rights to use the Macromedia Software. Although you own the disk on which the Macromedia Software is recorded, you do not become the owner of, and Macromedia retains title to, the Macromedia Product, and all copies thereof. All rights not specifically granted in this Agreement, including Federal and International Copyrights, are reserved by Macromedia.

6. Limited Warranties

(a) Macromedia warrants that, for a period of ninety (90) days from the date of delivery (as evidenced by a copy of your receipt): (i) when used with a recommended hardware configuration, the Macromedia Soft-ware will perform in substantial conformance with the documentation supplied as part of the Macromedia Product; and (ii) that the media on which the Macromedia Software is furnished will be free from defects in materials and workmanship under normal use. EXCEPT AS SET FORTH IN THE FOREGOING LIMITED

WARRANTY, MACROMEDIA DISCLAIMS ALL OTHER WARRANTIES, EITHER EXPRESS OR IMPLIED, INCLUDING THE WARRANTIES OF MERCHANTABILITY, FITNESS FOR A PARTICULAR PURPOSE AND NONINFRINGEMENT. IF APPLICABLE LAW IMPLIES ANY WARRANTIES WITH RESPECT TO THE MACROMEDIA PRODUCT, ALL SUCH WARRANTIES ARE LIMITED IN DURATION TO NINETY (90) DAYS FROM THE DATE OF DELIVERY. No oral or written information or advice given by Macromedia, its dealers, distributors, agents or employees shall create a warranty or in any way increase the scope of this warranty.

(b) SOME STATES DO NOT ALLOW THE EXCLUSION OF IMPLIED WARRANTIES, SO THE ABOVE EXCLUSION MAY NOT APPLY TO YOU. THIS WARRANTY GIVES YOU SPECIFIC LEGAL RIGHTS AND YOU MAY ALSO HAVE OTHER LEGAL RIGHTS WHICH VARY FROM STATE TO STATE.

7. Exclusive Remedy

Your exclusive remedy under Section 6 is to return the Macromedia Software to the place you acquired it, with a copy of your receipt and a description of the problem. Macromedia will use reasonable commercial efforts to supply you with a replacement copy of the Macromedia Software that substantially conforms to the documentation, provide a replacement for the defective media, or refund to you your purchase price for the Macromedia Software, at its option. Macromedia shall have no responsibility with respect to Macromedia Software that has been altered in any way, if the media has been damaged by accident, abuse or misapplication, or if the nonconformance arises out of use of the Macromedia Software in conjunction with software not supplied by Macromedia.

8. Limitations of Damages

(a) MACROMEDIA SHALL NOT BE LIABLE FOR ANY INDIRECT, SPECIAL, INCIDENTAL OR CONSEQUENTIAL DAMAGES (INCLUDING DAMAGES FOR LOSS OF BUSINESS, LOSS OF PROFITS, OR THE LIKE), WHETHER BASED ON BREACH OF CONTRACT, TORT (INCLUDING NEGLIGENCE), PRODUCT LIABILITY OR OTHERWISE, EVEN IF MACROMEDIA OR ITS REPRESENTATIVES HAVE BEEN ADVISED OF THE POSSIBILITY OF SUCH DAMAGES AND EVEN IF A REMEDY SET FORTH HEREIN IS FOUND TO HAVE FAILED OF ITS ESSENTIAL PURPOSE.

(b) Macromedia's total liability to you for actual damages for any cause whatsoever will be limited to the greater of $500 or the amount paid by you for the Macromedia Software that caused such damages.

(c) SOME STATES DO NOT ALLOW THE LIMITATION OR EXCLUSION OF LIABILITY FOR INCIDENTAL OF CONSEQUENTIAL DAMAGES, SO THE ABOVE LIMITATION OR EXCLUSION MAY NOT APPLY TO YOU.

9. Basis of Bargain

The limited warranty, exclusive remedies and limited liability set forth above are fundamental elements of the basis of the bargain between Macromedia and you. Macromedia would not be able to provide the Macromedia Software on an economic basis without such limitations.

10. Government End Users

The Macromedia Product is "Restricted Computer Software."

RESTRICTED RIGHTS LEGEND

Use, duplication, or disclosure by the Government is subject to restrictions as set forth in subparagraph (c)(1)(ii) of the Rights in Technical Data and Computer Software clause at DFARS 252.227-7013. Manufacturer: Macromedia, Inc., 600 Townsend, San Francisco, CA 94103

11. General

This Agreement shall be governed by the internal laws of the State of California. This Agreement contains the complete agreement between the parties with respect to the subject matter hereof, and supersedes all prior or contemporaneous agreements or understandings, whether oral or written. All questions concerning this Agreement shall be directed to: Macromedia, Inc., 600 Townsend, San Francisco, CA 94103, Attention: Chief Financial Officer.